CAROB COOKBOOK

TRICIA
HAMILTON

Sunstone Press
Santa Fe, New Mexico

Photo on Cover: Mocha Fudge Cake

First Edition

Printed in the United States of America

Library of Congress Cataloging in Publication Data:

Hamilton, Tricia, 1951-
    Carob cookbook / Tricia Hamilton. – 1st. ed.
        p.   cm.
    Includes index.
    ISBN: 0-86534-135-4 : $10.95
    1. Cookery (Carob) I. Title.
TX814.5.C35H36 1989   89-4569
641.6′446–dc20   CIP

Published in 1990 by SUNSTONE PRESS
                Post Office Box 2321
                Santa Fe, NM 87504-2321 / USA

CONTENTS

INTRODUCTION

There are more and more products on supermarket shelves trending towards less fat, less sugar, lower calories, no caffiene, no preservatives, etc., etc., etc. And chocolate is one of the products we are leaning away from. Chocolate causes allergic reactions in some people, it contains caffiene, is high in saturated fat, it takes a lot of sweetening to override its bitterness and is usually high calorie. But lets face it, we love chocolate.

Carob, on the other hand, is naturally sweet, has fiber content, low fat, contains vitamins and minerals, including calcium and has no caffiene. And, it tastes similar to chocolate, if prepared properly. Whether you wish to cut down on chocolate, eliminate it from your diet, or just add carob for its healthy benefits, you can still enjoy special treats with a rich chocolaty flavor.

But what is carob and where does it come from? Oh, but of course ?? It is a cocoa-brown powder and it comes from the health store!!!

But seriously, if curiosity has got you, carob is derived from the Ceratonia Siliqua tree (Luguminosae, pea family). It is native to the Mediterranean Sea shores. It also grows in hot climates such as California, Arizona and Florida. The Ceratonia Siliqua tree can reach 50 feet in height. The trees bear flat leathery pods 3 to 12 inches long which contain 5 to 15 sweet pulp or seeds. When mature, the pods drop from the tree. After being gathered, the pods are split and the seeds separated out. The pods are then dried to a leathery texture and ground into powder. This is known as raw carob powder. This raw powder has a rather strange taste. But after it is roasted it turns a reddish brown with a pleasing taste. Carob is more commonly known and sold as a pure roasted powder. It can also be purchased in candy bars, chips and dry beverage mix. But before you buy a carob candy bar and base your opinion of the flavor of carob on that, try some of the recipes in this cookbook. The pure, roasted, powdered form of carob is the one used in these recipes. Carob chips are also used in a few.

So, here is my collection of recipes made with carob — taste pleasing to even those hard to please. Carob is midly sweet and does not need a lot of heavy sweetners. Although some desserts rely on a certain amount of sweetening agent to obtain lightness or texture, you will find that by using carob you can use measurably less sweetners and get perfect results. The added nutrition it gives desserts plus its delicate chocolate flavor is just too good to resist!

Now, carob will not cook and mix exactly like chocolate. Even though the taste is similar to that of chocolate, the two are different in the way they react with some ingredients. Not to worry! These recipes were developed to make carob easy to work with in mixing and baking, plus give the taste we are looking for. By following the simple instructions in the recipes and notes and reading the helpful tips, you will be making creamy pies, perfect cookies, light cakes and velvety frostings with carob. Your delicious and healthier desserts will win you compliments from family and friends.

If you are concerned that your family may not be ready for an instant switch from chocolate to carob, you can begin by using part carob powder and part cocoa powder to equal the amount specified in the recipe, using more carob powder than cocoa powder. Slowly decrease the amount of cocoa powder, as you progress into carob baking. This small change will not effect the mixing or cooking in the recipes. Your family will readily accept the carob flavor.

Many cooks like to use baking squares. I have developed my own version of baking squares, using carob. These squares are fully described in the chapter "Carob Baking Squares".

I have included a variety of recipe choices. Some of us prefer using whole wheat flour and honey, while others would rather use "all purpose" or unbleached flour and granulated sugar. I have included a wide variety of both types of cooking preferences. They are all equally good. You will get pleasing results you and your family will enjoy with any and all the recipes you choose.

The recipes or any information in this cookbook are not intended for medicinal uses whatsoever; nor to take the place of any type of medical or physician advice. The recipes were developed simply as desserts and snacks as you would use any similar desserts recipe.

H A P P Y   B A K I N G !

TIPS & ALTITUDE ADJUSTMENTS

Special Tips to Remember:

• Always grease pans with solid shortening or butter. Non-stick cooking sprays work well for cookies and pies. If using cooking sprays in cake pans, flour generoulsy to prevent sticking.

• When measuring carob powder or flour, when sifting is not stated, lightly spoon into measure for accurate measure.

• If carob is lumpy in container, when purchased, always sift.

• Glass baking dishes cook faster than metal pans. Lower baking temperature by 25 degrees when baking with glass.

• If recipe states: butter or margarine, room temperature, do not melt. This can affect your mixing and or the finished results.

• Read through recipes before you begin preparing them. You may find something you were not expecting! Like a chilling period or standing time you hadn't planned on. Or even one or more of the ingredients at room temperature, instead of straight from the cold refrigerator; which will make mixing much easier on you.

• There are special notes and hints throughout this cookbook, to help make your baking and mixing easier. Please take a second to notice them. They are for you.

• Another fact to consider is the wrong oven temperature can affect the things you bake. First, it is a good idea to check 'your' oven temperatures. A small oven thermometer can be purchased at most supermarkets or cooking shops. The cost of one of these thermometers is very inexpensive. If your oven is cooking hotter than the temperature you've set it at, you need to set the baking temperature lower, accordingly. If it is cooking cooler than the temperature at which you set it, you need to set it hotter, accordingly.

• Cooking times stated in recipes usually give a short time period; such as 8-10 minutes or 35-40 minutes, etc. Use the shortest time for checking the proper baking time. If not quite done, carefully close oven door and continue baking up to longer given time. In most cases these times are sufficient. Because of situations beyond the author's control, occasionally a longer or shorter baking time may be required. Some of these situations may have to do with humidity, kitchen temperatures, oven temperatures, baking pans themselves or extreme altitude difference.

Altitude Adjustments:

Altitude and temperature changes can affect some of the foods you bake. As a rule, cakes, cooked frostings and candies are sensitive to altitude. Following, is some information pertaining to altitude differences and temperatures. If you live at a high altitude, this section may help to get your cakes lighter and candy that always sets up.

Do you notice that your baked foods are not always what you feel they could be, and you follow the recipe instruction carefully. It may be necassary, in your area, to use altitude adjustments. If this applies to you, you will soon learn exact adjustments that are best for your elevation.

These adjustments are to give you a general guide from 3,000 to 8,000 feet elevation:

Baking:

Increase oven temperature by 25 degrees above 3,000 feet.
Increase liquid ingredients by adding:

1 tablespoon   to each cup — 3,000-4,500 feet elevation
2 tablespoons to each cup — 4,500-5,500 feet elevation
3 tablespoons to each cup — 5,500-6,500 feet elevation
4 tablespoons each cup — 6,500-8,000 feet elevation

Decrease sugar:

1 tablespoon   each cup — 3,000-4,500 feet elevation
2 tablespoons each cup — 4,500-6,000 feet elevation
3 tablespoons each cup — 6,000-8,000 feet elevation

Decrease leavening, (baking powder and soda)
1/8 teaspoon each tsp. — 3,000-5,500 feet elevation
1/4 teaspoon each tsp. — 5,500-8,000 feet elevation

Yeast risen breads and pastries will rise faster at high altitudes.

You can check with the public service company in your area and usually request a completed guide in cooking and baking adjustments for your area.

Boiling:

At sea level, boiling point for water is 212 degrees F.
Boiling point at 2,000 feet elevation is 208 degrees F.
Boiling point at 5,000 feet elevation is 203 degrees F.
Boiling point at 10,000 feet elevation is 194 degrees F.

At higher elevations, liquids require longer cooking times because liquids boil faster at lower temperatures.

Candy & Syrups: Soft ball stage

	sea level — 236 degrees F.
	3,000 ft. — 230 degrees F.
	5,000 ft. — 226 degrees F.
	7,000 ft. — 222 degrees F.
	8,000 ft. — 218 degrees F.

Oven Temperatures

Warm	200-250 degrees F.
Slow	250-325 degrees F.
Moderate	325-375 degrees F.
Hot	375-450 degrees F.
Very Hot	450-500 degrees F.

CAROB BAKING SQUARES

1
CAROB
BAKING SQUARES

This is my version of baking squares and I have developed several versions, each with its own qualities.

When you start making and using carob squares, you will notice how easy they are to use. For instance, other baking squares must be melted down from a hard, solid form. The carob baking squares, on the other hand, only need to come to room temperature from the refrigerator or freezer. This in itself tells you that the fat or oil you make your Carob Squares with will be healthier and more easily digested than the hard solid fat in other baking squares.

As you begin using carob powder, you may notice, as with any dry powder, it can occasionally be difficult to dissolve. The carob baking squares were developed for easier, smoother mixing in your recipes. Your batters and mixtures will be smooth and creamy. Use a small to medium bowl and a fork to stir together the ingredients. This will moisten the carob powder and make mixing your carob baking squares very easy. Occasional notes, hints and helpful tips have been provided to make your mixing and baking procedures go easily and trouble free.

The carob baking squares only take a short time to prepare. Making sure you have the proper ingredients on hand, prepare several recipes for carob baking squares. Freeze as directed in the basic freezing methods & container suggestion section. Later, when you are ready to mix up a cake, or make the children some cookies, you'll already have an assortment of healthy baking squares in your freezer.

If you wish to substitute one type carob square for another, be careful, for the recipes were developed with the carob square called for in each recipe. Try and only substitute common or like carob squares, if you must substitute.

All ingredients in these recipes are available in most grocery stores and health food stores. If your favorite market or health store does not carry something needed, ask the store manager if he or she could order it. They are usually happy to help.

This chapter has been fun to develop and work with. Realizing that you may not always want to use the carob baking squares in your baking, they are not included in all the recipes. The choice is yours.

FREEZING & STORAGE METHODS:

You can store carob baking squares in your refrigerator for about two weeks. For a convenient way to keep carob baking squares on hand, you can freeze them. They will keep well in your freezer for two or three months. At normal room temperature it will take about 1 hour for your carob baking squares to thaw or come close enough to room temperature to use in your recipe. They can be removed from freezer the night before and placed in the refrigerator. It will then take 15 to 30 minutes to soften to room temperature.

Each individual carob baking square will equal a 1 ounce measure all through the recipes in this cookbook. For instance, if a recipe calls for 3 carobutter squares, you will use 3 - 1 ounce squares. (1 square = 1 ounce)

Each carob baking square recipe will make 10-12 ounces (1 & 1/4 to 1 & 1/2 cups). Measure each mixture you make so you will know exactly how many squares you will be making from each recipe.

Note: Carob powder is very fine and it settles easily. The measures stated in the recipes should be stirred and lightly spooned or even sifted into measuring cups. Do not tap or shake. If not measured lightly, your mixture may be dry. The carob powder measurements are crucial. The carob baking square mixtures are thick and may seem hard to stir, but you should get a smooth moist mixture from each recipe. The mixtures are thick so the carob powder can be as concentrated as possible in your carob squares and still have a baking square you can work with.

The squares will freeze very firm to hard except for the caroboil square, which stay soft when frozen. Caroboil squares should be placed in 1 ounce cups; or place in sealed containers and measure needed portion for each recipe, returning remaining mixture to freezer.

HELPFUL TIPS:

• If your mixture equals 12 ounces, (1 & 1/2 cups), you will cut 12 equal squares or pour mixture into 12 - 1 ounce cups.

• A 1/8 cup measure equals 1 ounce.

• To speed thawing time, place squares in bowl and place bowl over another bowl which is half filled with very hot water. Squares will soften very quickly. *Don't* heat in saucepan over stove top to soften or carob will start to cook.

• Bold print appearing in recipes indicates that the recipe can be found in this cookbook, under chapter heading in which it applies.

CONTAINER SUGGESTIONS:

One Ounce Containers:

- 1 ounce cups available at speciality cookware shops.
- The 1 ounce cups some beverage mixes come in.
- Standard plastic ice trays — each ice cube equals 1 oz.
- Tiny tart pans — each cup equals 1 ounce. (minature muffin cups)

To freeze: Spoon mixture evenly into each cup. Place on a tray and place in freezer 1 to 2 hours to harden. Transfer to freezer bags or plastic, freezer containers. (Except for caroboil squares, which stay soft and must be left in cups and placed in flat bottomed freezer containers, standing upright.)

To thaw: Remove amount needed from freezer. May be placed in bowl or left in containers. Let stand at room temperature about 1 hour.

Large Square Freezer Containers:

8 X 8 inch square dish
4 x 8 inch loaf pan
5 X 9 inch loaf pan
3 X 7 inch loaf pan
6 X 6 inch plastic freezer container

Spoon mixture evenly into container which has been lightly greased with butter or non-stick spray coating. Cut into equal 1 ounce squares; diagrams below.

For 12 ounces, (1 & 1/2 cups), cut 3 equal strips one direction, then 4 equal strips the other direction. Or cut once down center, then cut 6 equal strips across side. Cover, place in freezer 1 to 2 hours. Squares can be covered tightly and left in dish. Or transfer to freezer bags or freezer containers. Each square can be wrapped separately in small 4 inch squares of wax paper if desired. Label and freeze.

For 10 ounces, (1 & 1/4 cups), cut down center one direction, then in 5 equal strips the other direction. Cover and freeze as above.

12 squares, (ounces)   10 squares, (ounces)

CAROBUTTER SQUARES

These squares are made with butter or margarine which has come to room temperature. Never melt the butter or margarine or you may not be able to completely mix it into the carob powder.

Carobutter Squares:

1 cup butter or margarine, room temperature
1 cup carob powder, lightly spooned or sifted

Using a fork, stir carob powder into soft, not melted, butter or margarine. Mix till moistened and mixture is smooth. Measure your mixture. Spoon into desired containers, label, seal and prepare for freezer, or refrigerator.
Yields 10 to 12 ounces

Honey Carobutter Squares:

3/4 cup butter or margarine, room temperature
1/3 cup honey
1 cup carob powder, lightly spooned or sifted

In small bowl combine butter or margarine and honey. Mix till smooth. Add carob powder and stir till well mixed and smooth. Measure. Spoon into desired containers, label, seal and prepare for freezer, or refrigerator.
Yields 10 to 12 ounces

Sweet Carobutter Squares:

1 cup butter or margarine, room temperature
1 & 1/2 tblsp. vanilla extract
1/3 cup powdered sugar
1 cup carob powder, lightly spooned or sifted

In small bowl, mix together butter, vanilla and powdered sugar till creamy. Stir in carob powder till smooth. Measure. Spoon into desired containers, label, seal and prepare for freezer, or refrigerator.
Yields 10 to 12 ounces

CAROBOIL SQUARES

The caroboil squares are made with vegetable oil and will give moist results in recipes. For those who prefer vegetable oil to other fats in their diets, these are for you.

►

Caroboil Squares:

1 cup vegetable oil
2 & 1/4 - 2 & 1/2 cups carob powder, lightly spoon or sift

In a glass bowl combine oil and 2 cups carob powder. Stir till well mixed. Add just enough remaining carob powder to make thick smooth paste. Measure. Spoon into desired containers, label, seal, prepare for freezer.
Yields 10 to 12 ounces

Honey Caroboil Squares:

1 cup vegetable oil
1 & 1/2 cups carob powder, lightly spooned or sifted
1/4 cup honey

Place oil in small bowl; stir in carob powder. Mix well to dissolve carob. Add honey, stir. Mixture will be thin and thicken as you stir. Stir to smooth consistency. Don't over stir. Measure. Spoon into desired container, label, prepare for freezer.
Yields 10 to 12 ounces

Sweet Caroboil Squares:

1 & 1/2 - 1 & 3/4 cups carob powder, lightly spoon or sift
1/2 cup powdered sugar
1 cup vegetable oil
1 & 1/2 tblsp. vanilla extract

Combine 1 cup of carob powder and powdered sugar. Add oil and vanilla; mix well. Stir in just enough of remaining 1/2 to 3/4 cup carob powder to make a thick, smooth paste like mixture. Measure. Spoon into desired containers, seal, label, prepare for freezer.
Yeilds 10 to 12 ounces

CAROB OILBUTTER SQUARES

These carob squares are made with both vegetable oil and butter, or margarine. This gives the moistness of oil, plus the flavor and texture of butter. Along with the health benefits of vegetable oil.

Carob Oilbutter Squares

1 & 1/3 cups carob powder, lightly spooned or sifted
1/2 cup butter or margarine, room temperature
1/2 cup vegetable oil, room temperature

In small bowl, combine butter and oil; mix till smooth and lemony colored. With fork, stir in carob powder to a thick, smooth paste. Measure the mixture.

►

Spoon into desired containers; label; prepare for freezer.
Yields 10 to 12 ounces

Honey Carob Oilbutter Squares

1 & 1/4 cups carob powder, lighty spooned of sifted
1/3 cup vegetable oil, room temperature
1/3 cup butter or margarine, room temperature
1/3 cup honey

Stir oil and butter together till smooth. Slowly add and stir in carob powder, using fork to mix. When smooth and creamy add honey; mix till smooth. Measure. Spoon into desired containers; label; prepare for freezer.
Yields 10 to 12 ounces

Sweet Carob Oilbutter Squares

1 & 1/4 cups carob powder, lightly spooned or sifted
1/2 cup vegetable oil, room temperature
1/2 cup butter or margarine, room temperature
1 & 1/2 tlbsp. vanilla extract
1/3 cup powdered sugar

Combine vegetable oil and butter in small bowl; stir with fork till smooth. Stir in carob powder and mix till smooth and thick. Add vanilla and powdered sugar, stir in. Measure. Spoon into desired containers, label, freeze.
Yields 10 to 12 ounces

LITE CAROB SQUARES

Lite Carob Squares are just what they imply. They are made with water instead of oil or butter.

Lite Carob Squares:

2 cups carob powder, lightly spooned or sifted
1 cup water

In small bowl, stir carob powder into water. Mix till carob powder is dissolved. Mixture will be thick paste. Measure. Spoon into desired containers, seal, label, prepare for freezer.
Yields 10 to 12 ounces

Honey Lite Carob Squares:

1/3 cup honey
3/4 cup water
1 & 3/4 cups carob powder, lightly spooned or sifted

In small bowl, combine honey and water. Mix together. Stir in carob powder till

►

smooth and thick. Measure your mixture. Spoon into desired container, seal, label, prepare for freezer.
Yeilds 10 to 12 ounces

Sweet Lite Carob Squares:

1 & 3/4 cups carob powder, lightly spooned or sifted
1 cup water
1 & 1/2 tblsp. vanilla extract
1/3 cup powdered sugar

Stir carob powder into water, using fork to mix. Mixture will be very thick. Add vanilla and powdered sugar; mix well till dry ingredients are dissolved. Should be smooth paste. Measure. Spoon into desired containers, seal, label, prepare for freezer.
Yields 10 to 12 ounces

FLAVORED CAROB BAKING SQUARES

To give you a special way to have your favorite flavors right in the carob squares, this recipe section shows you some of the flavors which go best with the flavor of carob and how to add them to your squares.

Flavored Carob Baking Squares:

1 carob baking square recipe, your choice
1 & 1/2 tblsp. flavor extract, one of following:

Vanilla extract	Orange extract
Almond extract	Mint extract
Cherry extract	

Add desired flavor extract to liquid portion of recipe. Proceed as directed in recipe choice. Label accordingly, place in containers, seal and freeze.

EXAMPLE: Cherry Caroboil Squares:
      1 recipe caroboil squares
      1 & 1/2 tblsp. cherry extract

Place vegetable oil and cherry extract in bowl. Add 2 cups carob powder, stir till well mixed. Add just enough of remaining carob powder to make thick, smooth paste. Measure. Spoon into desired containers, label, seal, prepare for freezer.

These flavored squares will give you variety in your recipes. As you use them to replace other carob squares, exchange like or common squares for best results in your finished product. You can add or change flavors in your recipes.

Note: I use only pure extracts in the recipes, as the flavor is superior to artifical flavoring.

CAROB CREAM SQUARES

These squares are made with cream cheese. You can make them with regular cream cheese or light cream cheese, not whipped. The creaminess in these squares make great frostings and fillings.

Carob Cream Squares:

8 ounce pkg. cream cheese, room temperature
1/4 cup honey
1 tblsp. vanilla extract
1 cup carob powder

In small, deep bowl, beat cream cheese together with honey and vanilla. Beat till smooth. Stir in carob powder. Mixture will be very thick. Press into desired freezer containers, seal, label, prepare for freezer.
Yields 10 to 12 ounces

SPICY CAROB SQUARES

Carob and spices go well together. Here is a carob baking square with just enough spiciness to be nice!!

1/2 cup butter, room temperature
1/2 cup molasses
2 tsp. ground cinnamon
1/2 tsp. ground ginger
1/4 tsp. ground cloves
1/2 cup carob powder

In small bowl, beat butter and molasses together till caramel colored and silky smooth. Stir in spices and carob powder till mixture is well mixed and creamy. Pour into desired containers, seal, label, prepare for freezer.
Yields 10 to 12 ounces

ADDITIONAL USES FOR CAROB BAKING SQUARES

Instant pudding mixes:

1 — 3.5. oz. pkg. instant pudding
1 carob baking square, your choice, room temperature

Prepare as directed on package, beating carob square in final beating process. For richer pudding beat in 2 sqs. Use flavored carob baking squares to add special flavors to your box puddings. ▶

Pudding & pie filling:

1 — 3.5 oz. package
1 carob baking square, your choice, room temperature.

Prepare as directed on package. When pudding has finished cooking, remove from heat. Stir in carob square. (for richer filling stir in 2 sqs.)

Frosting mixes:

Beat 2 to 3 carob baking squares, your choice, into any cream type frosting mixture, in final beating process.

Carob swirl ice cream:

1 quart vanilla ice cream
3 to 4 honey carob baking squares or sweet carob baking squares, room temperature.

Let ice cream stand at room temperature about 30 minutes to slightly soften, but not melt. Using knife, swirl carob squares into ice cream to desired swirl affect. Return to freezer.

Carob filled muffins or cupcakes:

To make 12 filled muffins or cupcakes
3 cold sweet carobutter squares
1 recipe or package for 12 cupcakes or muffins

Using sharp knife, cut each carob square into fourths. Grease 12 muffins cups. Filled each cup 1/3 full, place one of cut carob square pieces in center; place batter over top to 2/3 full. Bake as recipe directs.

Carob box cake:

1 standard yellow cake mix
3 carob baking squares, your choice, room temperature

Fold carob squares into cake batter. Pour into pan or pans as directed on package. Bake as directed.

Carob Marble Cake:

1 standard yellow cake mix
2 sweet carob baking squares or honey carob baking squares, room temperature

Prepare batter as directed on package. Pour into prepared pan or pans. Double layer cake — place 1 carob square in each pan with batter; carefully swirl through batter, not touching bottom or sides of pan. 13 x 9 inch cake — place both carob squares in pan over batter and carefully swirl into batter, not touching sides or bottom of pan.

Note: Carob will curdle if heated with milk at a high temperature unless milk has been scalded first. Even then do so with caution or you may risk ruining your mixture.

DOUBLE CAROB COOKIES recipe on page 21

2
COOKIES

DROP COOKIES

DOUBLE CAROB COOKIES

Crisp on the outside, tender and soft on inside

Preheat oven 375 degrees

1/2 cup soft butter or margarine
1/2 cup vegetable oil
1/2 cup brown sugar
1/2 cup granulated sugar
1/2 cup carob powder
1 tblsp. vanilla extract
1/2 tsp. salt
1 tsp. baking soda
2 eggs, slightly beaten
1 cup whole wheat flour
1 cup all purpose flour
1/2 cup raisins
1 cup chopped nuts
1 cup carob chips

In large bowl, combine butter, oil, sugars, carob powder, vanilla, salt and soda; mix till smooth. Stir in eggs to blend. Add flours, mix well. Stir in raisins, nuts and chips. Drop teaspoons full onto lightly greased cookie sheet. Bake in 375 degree oven 6-7 minutes; cookies will just begin to dry on top and center will be soft. Be careful not to over bake. Cool on racks.
Yields 5 & 1/2 dozen

CAROB MINT CHIP COOKIES

Chewy inside, crisp and tender outside

Preheat oven 375 degrees

4 **sweet carobutter squares,** room temperature	1 egg
1 cup brown sugar	1 & 2/3 cup all purpose flour
1/2 cup vegetable oil	1 tsp. baking soda
1 tsp. mint extract	dash salt
1 tsp. vanilla extract	1 cup carob mint chips
	1/2 cup chopped pecans

Beat carob squares, sugar and oil together till smooth. Add extracts and egg; beat well. Stir in flour, soda and salt. Mix till well blended. Stir in carob mint chips and pecans. Drop teaspoons full, 2 inches apart, onto lightly greased cookie sheet. Bake 375 degree oven 6-7 minutes. Cookies will puff up while baking; tops will be dry but soft to touch. While cookies cool, center will sink, making chewy centers.   Yields 4 dozen

Special Hint: To make jumbo cookies, use 1 heaping tablespoon cookie dough for each cookie. Place 3-4 inches apart on cookie sheet and bake on 350 degrees for 10 to 12 minutes or till done.

CAROB CHERRY COOKIES

Cherries and carob really hit it off good together

Preheat oven 375 degrees

1/2 cup butter or margarine, room temperature	1 cup all purpose flour
1/4 cup vegetable oil	1 cup whole wheat flour
2 **carob oilbutter squares**	dash salt
1 cup sugar	1 tsp. baking soda
2 eggs	1 cup carob chips
2 tsp. almond extract	1 cup chopped and drained maraschino cherries

Cream together butter, oil and carob squares in medium bowl. Beat in sugar; add eggs and almond extract. Stir in flours, salt and soda till well blended. Add carob chips and cherries. Drop 2 inches apart on greased cookie sheet. Bake at 375 degree 6-7 minutes, or till just set on top; don't over bake. Cool on racks.
      Yields 5 to 6 dozen cookies.

CAROB PEANUT BUTTER DREAM DROPS

Moist and rich fudgey flavored cookie mounds

Preheat oven 350 degrees

3/4 cup smooth peanut butter	1/2 cup sour cream
3/4 cup honey	1/2 tsp. baking soda
2 tblsp. vegetable oil	1 cup carob powder
1 egg	1/2 cup powdered sugar

In medium bowl combine peanut butter and honey; stir till smooth. Mix oil, egg and sour cream in till mixture is creamy. Stir in baking soda to dissolve. Stir the carob powder and powdered sugar into mixture till thoroughly combined. Batter will be very thick. Lightly grease a cookie sheet; drop teaspoons full 2 inches apart. Bake on 350 degrees 8-10 minutes, or till slightly puffed and tops just begin to crack. Remove from oven and let stand on cookie sheet 1 to 2 minutes. Carefully remove to racks to cool.
Yields 2 & 1/2 to 3 dozen

SWEET CAROB COOKIES

So good, you'll make them again and again

Preheat oven 350 degrees

1 egg	2 heaping tblsp. raw bran
1/2 cup vegetable oil	2 heaping tblsp. wheat germ
1 tsp. vanilla extract	1 tsp. baking soda
1 cup loosely packed	1/2 tsp. salt
brown sugar	1/2 cup chopped pecans
1/4 cup carob powder	1 cup carob chips
1 cup flour	

Beat egg, oil, vanilla and sugar till smooth. Add carob powder, flour, bran, wheat germ, soda and salt. Stir in pecans and carob chips. Drop heaping tablespoons onto lightly greased cookie sheet, 3 inches apart. Bake 8-12 minutes or till tops are puffed and just begin to dry. Cookies will be soft, if too soft let stand on cookie sheet 1 minute before removing to racks to cool. Cookie centers will sink.
Yields 2 Dozen

JUBILEE CHERRY COCONUT COOKIES

Coconut coated cookies are brownies on the inside

Preheat oven 350 degrees

4 **sweet carobutter squares,**
  room temperature
1/2 cup sweetened condensed
  canned milk
1 egg yolk
1 tsp. almond extract
2 tsp. cherry extract

1 cup all purpose flour
1 & 1/2 tsp. baking powder
2 cups flaked coconut, divided
1 cup chopped maraschino
  cherries, drained
1/2 cup chopped almonds

Beat carob squares with condensed milk, egg yolk, almond and cherry extracts till smooth. Stir in flour and baking powder till well mixed. Stir in 1 cup of coconut, cherries and almonds. Place remaining cup of coconut in shallow bowl. Drop teaspoons full, one at a time, into coconut; roll to coat, forming 1 & 1/4 inch balls. Place 2 inches apart on a greased cookie sheet. Bake at 350 degrees 10 minues, or till cookies are puffed and coconut is lightly browned.
  Yields 4 dozen cookies.

ORANGE & PINEAPPLE FILLED DROP COOKIES

Sweet cooked fruit filling in center of drop cookies — easy and special

Preheat oven 350 degrees

Fruit filling, recipe follows
1 egg
1/2 cup brown sugar
1/2 cup butter or margarine,
  partially melted
1/4 cup frozen orange juice
  concentrate, thawed, undiluted

1/2 tsp. orange extract
1/2 tsp. baking soda
dash salt
1 & 1/2 cups all purpose flour
1/3 cup carob powder

Prepare filling and set aside. Beat egg and sugar till light. While beating, blend in butter, juice and extract. Add soda. Stir in flour, salt and carob powder; mix well. Drop teaspoons full onto greased cookie sheet, 2 inches apart. Make a slight indention in center of each cookie; fill with about 1/2 teaspoon filling. Bake in 375 degrees oven 7-8 minutes.
Yields 2 & 1/2 dozen cookies

Fruit filling:

1/2 cup mandarine orange
  segments, drained
1/2 cup crushed pineapple

1/4 cup sugar
1 tsp cornstarch

►

Place all ingredients in small saucepan; cook on medium heat till bubbly and thick.

Variation: for raspberry filled drop cookies, follow previous recipe using raspberry jam instead of fruit filling.

ZUCCHINI CAROB COOKIES

A moist cookie with lots of flavor

Preheat oven 375 degrees

1/2 cup vegetable oil	1 & 1/2 tsp. baking soda
1/2 cup butter, or margarine,	2 tsp. cinnamon, ground
room temperature	1 tsp. nutmeg, ground
1 egg	1/2 tsp. salt
1 cup carob powder	1 cup grated zucchini
2 tsp. vanilla extract	1 cup coconut
1 cup brown sugar	1 cup chopped pecans
2 cups whole wheat flour	

In large mixing bowl blend oil and butter together; add egg. Beat in carob powder, brown sugar and vanilla till dark and thick. Stir in flour, soda, spices and salt, mix well. Add zucchini, coconut and pecans and stir in. Drop rounded teaspoons full, 2 inches apart on a lightly greased cookie sheet. Bake in 375 degree oven 8-10 minutes. Cookies will be dry on top but soft to touch. Cool on racks.   Yields 4 & 1/2 to 5 dozen cookies

CRUNCHY OATMEAL DROPS

Crunchy drop cookies that are not too sweet with good   flavor

1 cup all purpose flour	**2 carob cream squares,**
1 cup whole wheat flour	room temperature
1 tsp. baking soda	1/4 cup molasses, or dark corn syrup
1 tsp. cinnamon, ground	1/2 cup brown sugar
2 & 1/2 cups rolled oats	1 egg
1/2 cup butter, or margarine,	1/2 tsp. orange extract
room temperature	1/2 tsp. vanilla extract
1/2 cup vegetable oil,	Granulated sugar for sprinkling
room temperature	

Measure flours, soda, cinnamon and oats into large bowl. Stir to combine. In small bowl beat together butter, oil carob squares, molasses, sugar, egg and extracts till dark and smooth. Stir into dry ingredients in large bowl. Stir by hand,

▶

till well mixed. Drop from teaspoon about 2 inches apart onto lightly greased cookie sheet. Sprinkle tops of cookies with granulated sugar. Bake in 375 degree oven for 8-10 minutes or until slightly puffed and dry to top. Yields 4 dozen cookies.

Variation: for cunchy date oatmeal drops, add 1 cup of finely chopped dates to flour mixture in large bowl, stir to coat; make recipe as stated.

Helpful Hint: keep granulated sugar in spice bottle with sprinkle top, on your spice rack. A little sugar sprinkled over tops of cookies before baking will make cookies taste a lot sweeter without being heavily sweetened.

CAROB DATE 'N NUT MERINGUES

Sweet candy-like cookies with a little crunch!!

Preheat oven 300 degrees

1/3 cup honey
2 egg whites
1/4 tsp. cream of tartar
1 tsp. vanilla extract
1 cup chopped dates

2 cups coconut
1/2 cup chopped pecans
1 cup carob chips
1/3 cup carob powder

Heat honey to just under boiling; don't boil. Working quickly place egg whites in large mixing bowl of electric mixer and beat on high speed till foamy; add cream of tartar and beat to soft peaks. Slowly add hot honey in a fine stream, beat till glossy with soft set peaks but not dry; beat in vanilla. In separate bowl combine dates, coconut, pecans and carob chips. Stir the carob powder through coconut mixture to coat. Gently fold the coconut-carob mixture into the soft meringue. Lightly grease cookie sheet. Cut a piece of wax paper the size of cookie sheet and line bottom of cookie sheet with wax paper. Using a tablespoon, drop mounds of cookie mixture onto wax paper lined cookie sheet about 1 & 1/2 inches apart. Bake in preheated 300 degree oven for 20-25 minutes. Cookies will be set and appear dry on top. Carefully remove to racks to cool. Use a new piece of wax paper for each batch of cookies. (No need to grease bottom of cookie sheet again.) Store loosely covered in dry place. Yields 3 dozen cookies

14 KAROBT COOKIES

Carrot cookies can't get any better than this

Preheat oven 350 degrees

1 egg, (cold)	1 & 1/2 tsp. cinnamon, ground
1/2 cup vegetable oil, (cold)	1 tsp. grated orange rind
2/3 cup honey	dash salt
1 tsp. orange extract	1/2 cub bran, raw
1 cup whole wheat flour	1 & 1/2 cups finely grated carrots
1/2 cup carob powder	1 cup chopped pecans
1 tsp. baking soda	

In medium mixing bowl beat egg, oil and honey till thickens. Add extract, flour, carob powder, soda, cinnamon, orange rind and salt, mix well. Stir in bran, carrots and pecans to blend. Drop heaping teaspoons full 2 inches apart on to a lightly greased cookie sheet. Bake in 350 degree oven for 10-12 minutes or till puffed and set. Cool on racks. Frost with Cookie Cream Frosting, below.
Yields 4 dozen cookies

Cookie Cream Frosting:

6 oz. cream cheese,	2 tblsp. sour cream
room temperature	1/4 to 1/3 cup powdered milk
1/4 cup honey	1 tsp. vanilla extract

Mix together and beat till smooth. Chill before frosting cookies. Makes about 1/2 cup.

CAROB CHIP PEANUT BUTTER COOKIES

An easy drop cookie for peanut butter lovers

Preheat oven 350 degrees

1/2 cup peanut butter	1 tsp. vanilla extract
1/4 cup vegetable oil	dash salt
1/2 cup butter or margarine,	1 tsp. baking soda
room temperature	1 cup all purpose flour
1/2 cup honey	1 cup whole wheat flour
1/2 cup brown sugar	1 cup carob chips
1 egg	

In medium bowl, beat together peanut butter, oil, butter, honey and brown sugar till smooth. Add egg, vanilla, salt and soda. Blend well. Mix in flours till well blended. Stir in carob chips. Drop teaspoons full, 2 inches apart, on a lightly greased cookie sheet. Bake in 350 degree oven 7 to 8 minutes or till just begin to brown.
Yields 4 dozen cookies

MINTY CAROB DROPS

A moist drop cookie with the refreshing flavor of mint

Preheat oven 375 degrees

4 lite carob squares,
    room temperature
1 cup butter or margarine
1/2 cup brown sugar
1/3 cup granulated sugar
1 tsp. mint extract
1 tsp. vanilla extract

1 egg
1 cup all purpose flour
1 cup whole wheat flour
1 tsp. baking soda
1 cup carob mint chips
1/2 cup chopped nuts

Blend butter and carob squares till light textured and creamy. Add sugars, extracts and egg; mix well. In separate bowl stir together flours and soda to combine. Stir into creamed mixture. Mix to blend. Add chips and nuts. Drop teaspoons full 2 inches apart on a greased cookie sheet. Bake in 375 degree oven 7-8 minutes. Cookies are done when just start to dry on top.
Yields 5 & 1/2 dozen cookies

ORANGE CAROB DROP COOKIES

So much flavor, healthy too!

Preheat oven 375 degrees

1/2 cup vegetable oil
1/2 cup honey
1 egg
1/4 cup frozen orange juice
    concentrate, thawed, undiluted
2 tblsp. grated orange peel
1 tsp. vanilla extract

1/2 cup carob powder
3/4 cup whole wheat flour
3/4 cup all purpose flour
1 tsp. baking soda
1 tsp. cinnamon
dash salt
1/2 cup chopped pecans
1/2 cup raisins

In medium bowl, beat together oil and honey. Add egg; blend in orange juice, grated peel, vanilla and carob powder. Beat smooth. In separate bowl stir together flours, soda, cinnamon and salt. Stir into carob mixture; mix well. Add pecans and raisins. Drop teaspoons full, 2 inches apart, onto greased cookie sheet. Bake at 375 degrees 6-7 minutes, being careful not to over bake.
Yields 4 dozen cookies

Special Hint: when grating peel from citrus fruit, grate only the outer orange part of peel. The white part of the peel is bitter with no flavor.

SHAPED COOKIES

CAROB CRISS CROSS COOKIES

A sweet, crunchy outside, chewy center and family favorite

Preheat oven 375 degrees

4 **caroboil squares,**	2 eggs
room temperature	1 tsp. baking soda
1/2 cup peanut butter	1 cup all purpose flour
1/2 cup sugar	1/4 cup additional sugar
1/2 cup brown sugar	

In medium bowl, mix together carob squares and peanut butter till smooth. Stir in the 1/2 cup sugar and 1/2 cup brown sugar. Add eggs and soda; stir well. Stir in flour. Shape teaspoons full of dough into 1 & 1/4 inch balls. Roll in additional 1/4 cup sugar, to coat. Place 2 inches apart on lightly greased cookie sheet. Flatten each cookie in criss-cross pattern with fork. Bake 375 degrees 6-8 minutes. Don't over bake.
Yields about 3 dozen cookies

RICH BROWNIE COOKIES

Sure to be a family favorite!

Preheat oven 375 degrees

1 cup all purpose flour	1 cup brown sugar
1 cup whole wheat flour	1/2 cup granulated sugar
1/2 cup carob powder	2 eggs
1 tsp. baking soda	1 tsp. vanilla extract
1/2 tsp. salt	1 tsp. almond extract
1 cup vegetable oil	

Stir together flours, carob powder, soda and salt in large bowl. Add oil; stir to mix. Blend in sugar, eggs and extracts. Using teaspoons full, form dough into 1 & 1/4 inch balls. Place 2 inches apart onto lightly greased cookie sheet. Bake in 375 degree oven 8 minutes, or till cookies are softly set. Let cookies stand on cookie sheet 1 minute longer; remove to racks to cool.
Yields 4 dozens cookies

Note: These cookies make a very moist batter. While shaping cookies, press dough together firmly to make balls.

PEPPERMINT CAROB SANDWICH COOKIES

Fancy little treats that are surprisingly easy to make

Preheat oven 350 degrees

1/2 cup softened butter
4 **sweet carobutter squares,**
   room temperature
2 eggs
1/4 tsp. peppermint extract
1/2 tsp. vanilla extract

3/4 tsp. baking powder
1/2 tsp. baking soda
1/4 tsp. salt
2 cups all purpose flour
Peppermint filling, recipe follows

Beat butter and carob squares till smooth. Blend in eggs and extracts. Beat till thickened. Stir in remaining ingredients, except filling, till well mixed. Make a mixture of 1/2 cup granulated sugar and 3 tablespoons flour for rolling dough on. Using 1/3 of dough at a time, sprinkle board with 1/3 of rolling mixture. Roll dough 1/8 to 1/4 inch thick. Cut out cookies with 2 inch cookie cutter. Place cookies on lightly greased cookie sheet, 2 inches apart. Bake in 350 degree oven 6-7 minutes. Cool on racks. Repeat with remaining dough. Spread 1 cookie with 1 teaspoon filling, place a 2nd cookie on top of filling, forming 1 filled cookie. Repeat with all cookies.
Yields 2 dozen filled cookies.

Peppermint Filling:

1/4 cup softened butter
1/4 cup softened cream cheese
1/2 cup **sweet powder**

(or powdered sugar)
1/4 tsp. peppermint extract

In small bowl, mix together all ingredients till smooth spreading consistency.

Note: If you prefer more filling in your cookies, double filling recipe and place 2 teaspoons filling in each cookie.

MOLASSES CAROB CRINKLES

Preheat oven 375 degrees

1/2 cup vegetable oil	sifted twice
1/2 cup brown sugar	1 & 1/2 tsp. baking soda
1/2 cup carob powder	2 tsp. cinnamon, ground
1 egg	1/2 tsp. nutmeg, ground
1/3 cup molasses	1/2 tsp. cloves, ground
2 cups whole wheat flour,	1/4 cup sugar, reserve for rolling

In medium bowl mix oil, brown sugar and carob powder. Add egg and molasses; beat in till creamy. Stir in remaining ingredients except the 1/4 cup sugar.

Form dough into 1 inch balls; roll in reserved sugar. Place 2 inches apart on lightly greased cookie sheet. Bake in 375 degree oven for 6-7 minutes or just till tops crack. Cool on racks.   Yields 3 & 1/2 dozen.

ORANGE CAROB CRACKLES

Preheat oven 350 degrees

1 cup vegetable oil	1 cup all purpose flour
2 eggs	1 cup rolled oats
2 tsp. orange extract	1 tsp. baking soda
3/4 cup brown sugar	1/2 tsp. salt
1/4 cup granulated sugar	1/2 cup raisins
1/2 cup carob powder	1/2 cup oat bran and
2 tblsp. grated orange rind	4 tblsp. powdered sugar
1/2 cup whole wheat flour	for rolling

Place oil, eggs and extract in small bowl, set aside. In medium mixing bowl place brown sugar, granulated sugar, carob powder and grated orange peel. All at once pour the egg-oil mixture into sugar mixture; beat till thick and smooth with electric mixer. By hand stir in flours, oats, soda and salt. Add raisins, stir in.

In small shallow bowl place the oat bran and the powdered sugar and mix together. Drop rounded teaspoons of dough into bran-sugar mixture and roll to coat; form 1 & 1/2 inch balls. Place 2 inches apart on a lightly greased cookie sheet, flatten slightly. Bake in 350 degree oven for 6-7 minutes. Cookies will be soft. Don't over-bake, they will continue to cook while cooling. Place on racks to cool. Yields 3 to 4 dozen cookies.

CHILLED DOUGH COOKIES

MINT FILLED TASSIES

Preheat oven 350 degrees

1/3 cup butter or margarine, room temperature	1 tsp. vanilla extract
	1 large egg yolk
1/3 cup sugar	3/4 cup all purpose flour
3 **carob oilbutter squares,**	2/3 cup finely chopped pecans
room temperature	Mint filling, recipe below

Cream butter and sugar till smooth, add the carob squares and vanilla. Beat in egg yolk. Stir in flour and pecans. Chill dough at least 1 hour.

Using teaspoons full shape dough into 1 inch balls and place in tiny tart pans*; making an indention in center of each cookie for filling. Fill each cookie center with 1 tsp. of filling. Bake in 350 degree oven, 12-15 minutes; till centers are puffed and set. Cool in pans 5 minutes. Remove from pan very carefully, as these cookies are fragile. Cool on racks.   Yields 2 dozen

Mint filling:

1/3 cup softened cream cheese	1/2 tsp. mint extract
1 egg white, room temperature	1 tblsp. butter or margarine
1/4 cup honey	1 tsp. cornstarch

Beat all ingredients thoroughly till smooth. Mixture will be slightly thin.

*Note: Tiny tart pans are also call minature muffin pans, with 1 & 1/2 inch muffin cups.

TINY TARTS WITH CAROB CENTERS

Minature muffin cups make these little cookies like tiny little pies

Preheat oven 325 degrees

3 ounces cream cheese	1 tsp. vanilla extract
1/2 cup butter or margarine,	1 cup all purpose flour
room temperature	1/2 cup **creamy carob filling,**
3 tblsp. brown sugar	(see frosting & filling section

Cream butter and cream cheese together. Add brown sugar and vanilla. Beat till sugar is dissolved. Stir in flour. Cover; chill dough 1 hour. Shape into 1 inch balls. Place each ball in lightly greased tiny tart pans, (minature 1 & 1/2 inch muffin cups). Press thumb print indention into center of each cookie, forming little cups. Fill each cup with 1 teaspoon filling. Bake in 325 degree oven 12 to 15 minutes or till centers are softly set. Let stand in pans 1 minute. Carefully remove to racks to cool.
Yields 2 dozen tiny tarts

CAROB COOKIE ASSORTMENT:
Top Left Clockwise: *MOLASSES CAROB CRINKLES, p. 31;
CAROB BUTTER BALLS, p. 42; CAROB CHERRY BONBONS,
p. 65; PEANUT BUTTER & CAROB FILLED COOKIES, p. 44; &
PEANUT BUTTER SURPRISE COOKIES, p. 43–44.*

CAROB BRAN SPICE CAKES recipe on page 60-61

MOCHA FUDGE CAKE, recipe on page 54

CAROB CREAM PIE recipe on page 81

TOP: *CAROB SWIRL ICE CREAM, recipe on page 19*
MIDDLE: *CAROB CREAM FREEZE, recipe on page 98*
BOTTOM: *BITTERSWEET SAUCE, on page 67, on ice cream*

CASTLEBERRY PIE recipe on page 79

CANDY ASSORTMENT:
Left to Right: COCONUTTY CANDY, p. 73; ALMOND CAROB CREAMS, p. 75; CHERRY SURPRISE FUDGE, P. 72; HONEY CAROB FUDGE, p. 73; RUM BALLS, p. 74; NO COOK FUDGE, p. 72; OL' FASHIONED FUDGE, p. 71

HONEY CAROB FUDGE recipe on page 73

CAROB LANE CAKE recipe on page 59

BREAD ASSORTMENT:
Top to Bottom: *CAROB NUT ROLL, p. 105; SPICY FILLED LOGS, p. 104; QUICK NUT ROLL, p. 107*

PEPPERMINT CAROB SANDWICH COOKIES, recipe on page 30

CHERRIES ON A CLOUD DESSERT recipe on page 97

CAROB SNAPS

Preheat oven 350 degrees

1/2 cup softened butter or margarine	1 tsp. ground cinnamon
1/4 cup powdered sugar	1 tsp. ground ginger
1/2 cup carob powder	1/2 tsp. baking soda
1 tblsp. vanilla extract	1/4 cup molasses
1 egg	1 cup all purpose flour
	Additional sugar for rolling

Place butter, powdered sugar, carob powder and vanilla into medium bowl; cream together. Add egg, cinnamon, ginger, soda and molasses; mix in well. Stir in flour. Cover; chill dough atleast 1 hour. Form chilled dough into 1 inch balls; roll in additional sugar to coat. Place 2 inches apart on lightly greased cookie sheet. Slightly flatten cookies with glass bottom. Bake 350 degrees. 6-7 minutes. Don't over bake.
Yields 2 & 1/2 to 3 dozen cookies

MOLDED PEANUT BUTTER CAROB COOKIES

Preheat oven 375 degrees

1/2 cup smooth peanut butter	1 egg
4 **carobutter squares,** room temperature	1 tsp. vanilla extract
2 tblsp. vegetable oil	3/4 cup all purpose flour
3/4 cup sugar	3/4 tsp. baking soda
	Additional sugar for rolling

In medium mixing bowl, beat together peanut butter, carob squares, oil and sugar. Beat till dark and creamy consistency. Blend in egg and vanilla. Stir in flour and soda. Mix well. Cover; chill dough 1 hour. Form chilled dough into 1 inch balls. Roll each ball in sugar to coat. Place on lightly greased cookie sheet, 2 inches apart. Slightly flatten each cookie with bottom of glass. (Dip glass in sugar if cookies stick) Bake in 375 degree oven 6-7 minutes, or till softly set.
Yields 3 dozen cookies

PEANUT BUTTER SUGAR BABIES

Sweet n' crispy on outside with rich chewy centers

Preheat oven 350 degrees

1 & 1/4 cups all purpose flour	1 cup brown sugar
1/2 cup carob powder	3/4 cup peanut butter
3/4 tsp. baking soda	1 egg
1/2 cup butter or margarine,	2 tsp. vanilla extract
room temperature	Additional granulated sugar,
1/4 cup vegetatble oil	for rolling
1/2 cup granulated sugar	

In small bowl combine flour, carob powder and soda; set aside. In large mixing bowl, beat together butter, oil, and sugars till creamy. Blend in peanut butter, egg and vanilla. Mix well. Add flour mixture to butter mixture. Stir till well combined; cover and chill one hour. Shape teaspoons full of dough into 1 & 1/4 inch balls. Roll balls in additional granulated sugar to coat. Place 2 inches apart on lightly greased cookie sheet. Bake in 350 degree oven 8-10 minutes or till tops just begin to crack; cookies will be soft. Let stand on cookie sheet 1 minute before removing to racks to cool.
Yields 4 & 1/2 to 5 dozen cookies

Special Note: These cookies will be very delicate when first removed from oven. Standing time will give cookies time to set but not over cook. Shorten baking time if cookies are not soft when taken from oven.

CAROB BUTTER BALLS

Crisp and buttery

Preheat oven 325 degrees

1/2 cup butter, or margarine,	1/4 cup powdered sugar
room temperature	1 tsp. vanilla extract
4 **honey carobutter squares,**	1 & 1/4 cups all purpose flour
room temperature	2/3 cup finely chopped pecans

Cream butter and carob squares till dark and smooth. Beat in powdered sugar and vanilla. Stir in flour. Add pecans. Cover and chill 30 to 60 minutes. When chilled shape into 1 inch balls. Place 2 inches apart on ungreased cookie sheet. Bake in 325 degree oven, 12-15 minutes. Cool on racks. Roll cooled cookies in additional powdered sugar, or Sweet Powder (see index for recipe).
Yields 3 dozen

CAROB CHERRY BON BONS

Crunchy nut coating and a cherry in the middle; these cookies are great after dinner with coffee.

Preheat oven 350 degrees

1 cup softened butter
   or margarine
3/4 cup brown sugar
1 egg
1 tsp. vanilla extract
1/2 tsp. almond extract
1 cup all purpose flour

3/4 cup whole wheat flour
1/3 cup carob powder
3/4 tsp. baking soda
dash salt
33 maraschino cherries,
   cut in half
1 cup finely chopped almonds

Beat butter and sugar till light. Add egg and extracts; blend in. Stir in flours, carob powder, soda and salt. Cover and chill 1 hour. Wrap teaspoons full of chilled dough around each cherry half. Place finely chopped almonds in shallow dish; roll each cookie ball in nuts to coat. Place on lightly greased cookie sheet, 2 inches apart. Bake in 350 degree oven 10-12 minutes or till very lightly browned.   Yields 65 cookies

PEANUT BUTTER SURPRISE COOKIES

Filled bon-bon type cookies

Preheat oven 350 degrees

6 ounces cream cheese,
   room temperature
1/2 cup butter or margarine,
   room temperature
2/3 cup sugar
1 & 1/2 tsp. vanilla extract
1 large egg

1 & 1/2 cups all purpose flour
1 tsp. baking powder
1/2 cup carob powder
Peanut Butter Filling,
   recipe follows
Carob Icing, recipe follows

In medium bowl, beat cream cheese and butter till creamy. Add sugar and vanilla, beat smooth. Blend in egg. In a separate bowl, combine flour, baking powder and carob powder, stir together to combine. Spoon dry ingredients into creamed mixture, stirring to mix well. Cover and chill for 1 hour. Prepare filling. When chilled, shape teaspoons full of dough into 1 & 1/4 inch balls, handling dough gently. Make an indention in center of each ball; fill with 1/2 to 1 teaspoon filling. Pinch dough close over filling to seal. Place on lightly greased cookie sheet, 2 inches apart. Bake in 350 degree oven 8-10 minutes. Cool on racks. When cool ice cookies with Carob Icing.
Yields 3 dozen

▶

Peanut Butter Filling: 1/3 cup smooth peanut butter   2 tblsp. carob powder
3 tblsp. honey   1 tblsp. melted butter

Stir together by hand till smooth; mixture will be thick.

Carob Icing: **2 honey carobutter squares,**   3/4 cup powdered sugar
room temperature   2 tblsp. milk, (or cream)

In small bowl mix all ingredients till velvety smooth.

PEANUT BUTTER AND CAROB FILLED COOKIES

Delicate wafer cookies with creamy peanut butter carob filling

Preheat oven 375 degrees

1/2 cup butter or margarine,   1/2 cup whole wheat flour
room temperature   3/4 cup all purpose flour
1/2 cup powdered sugar   1/2 tsp. baking soda
1 tblsp. lemon juice   dash salt
1 tsp. vanilla extract   **peanut butter carob filling,**
1 egg   recipe follows

Beat butter and powdered sugar till light. Add lemon juice, vanilla and egg. Beat well. Stir in flours, soda and salt. On 12 inch piece of wax paper, shape dough into an even roll about 1 & 1/2 inches in diameter and 8 to 10 inches long. Wrap wax paper around roll to seal. Chill several hours or overnight. When chilled, slice in 1/8 inch slices; place on lightly greased cookie sheet 1 & 1/2 to 2 inches apart. Bake in 375 degree oven 6-7 minutes, or till lighly brown-ed. Remove cookies to racks to cool; cookies will be delicate and crisp. Cool completely. Prepare filling. Coat bottom side of one cookie with rounded teas-poon of filling; place second cookie on top — bottom sides of cookies to fill-ing, forming 1 filled cookie. Continue filling all cookies.
Yields 20 filled cookies

Peanut Butter Carob Filling:

3 sweet carobutter squares,   4 tblsp. smooth peanut butter
room temperature   3 tblsp. honey

Place all filling ingredients in small bowl. Mix together till creamy smooth. Makes about 2/3 cup.

Variation: for carob cream filled cookies using above cookie dough, fill with:

Carob Cream Filling: 4 **carob cream squares,** room temperature.
3 to 4 tblsp. honey
1/2 tsp. vanilla extrat

Mix all filling ingredients till smooth.

BARS & BROWNIES

COCONUT PECAN BARS

These bar cookies are tasty and easy to make; the coconut topping is baked right on top of cookies.

Preheat oven 350 degrees

1/2 cup vegetable oil	1/2 tsp. baking soda
1/2 cup honey	1 tsp. baking powder
2 **lite carob squares,**	dash salt
room temperature	2 cups whole wheat flour
1 egg	1 cup chopped dates
1 tsp. grated orange peel	Coconut Topping, recipe follows
1 tsp. orange extract	

In medium bowl, beat oil and honey, till well blended. Add carob squares. Beat in next 7 ingredients to blend. Stir in dates. Spread cookie batter evenly into well greased 10 x 14 x 1 inch baking sheet. (9 x 13 inch cake pan will work.) Prepare Coconut Topping. Spoon Coconut Topping evenly over top of cookie dough in pan. Bake in 350 degree oven for 20-25 minutes or till lightly browned. Cool 10 minutes; cut in 2 inch squares.
Yields 35 bars

Coconut Topping:

1 egg	1/2 cup chopped pecans
1/3 cup maple syrup	1 cup coconut

Beat egg and maple syrup together. Stir in the pecans and coconut.

YOGURT COOKIE SQUARES

Simple cookie squares to serve with ice cream or fruit

Preheat oven 350 degrees

1/4 cup melted butter
    or margarine, cooled
1/2 cup sugar
1 egg
1/3 cup plain yogurt
1 tsp. vanilla extract

1/2 tsp. baking powder
1/4 tsp. baking soda
1 cup flour
1/2 recipe **semi-sweet**
    creamy carob frosting,
    (see section on frostings)

In medium bowl stir melted butter and sugar together. Add egg, mixing till smooth. Stir in yogurt and vanilla till blended. Mix in baking powder and soda. Stir in flour just to make smooth batter. Spread in greased 9 x 13 x 1 inch baking sheet. Bake 350 degrees 15-20 minutes; edges will brown and center will test done. Cool completely. Prepare Semi Sweet Creamy Carob Frosting; spread a thin coating evenly over cookies. Cut in squares.
Yields 24-28 squares

ORANGE & CAROB ZUCCHINI BARS

Nutritionally packed bars that taste as good as they are healthy

Preheat oven 325 degrees

1 cup raisins
1/2 cup chopped dates
1/2 cup chopped prunes
1/3 cup orange juice
    concentrate, undiluted
2 eggs
1/2 cup vegetable oil
3/4 cup brown sugar
1/2 cup honey
1 tblsp. vanilla extract

1/2 cup carob powder
1 & 1/2 cup whole wheat flour
2 tsp. cinnamon, ground
1/2 tsp. nutmeg, ground
1/4 tsp. cloves, ground
1 & 1/2 tsp. baking soda
1/2 tsp. salt
1 cup grated zucchini
1 cup chopped nuts

In a small bowl combine the raisins, dates, prunes and orange juice, set aside. In large bowl beat eggs, oil and sugar on medium speed on electric mixer. Add honey slowly while continuing to beat on medium speed. Blend in vanilla and carob powder beat till creamy. Stir in flour, spices, soda and salt till well mixed. By hand stir in zucchini, nuts and the orange-fruit mixture. Spoon into well greased and floured 13 x 9 inch baking pan; spread evenly to sides of pan. Bakes in 325 degree oven 35 to 40 minutes or till tests done in center. Cool completely and cut into bars.   Yields about 40 bars

Note: These bars are best if covered and placed in refrigerator overnight to enhance flavors.

TRADITIONAL BROWNIES

Preheat oven 350 degrees

1/2 cup carob powder
1/2 cup butter or margarine,
   partially melted
1 cup sugar
2 eggs

1 tsp. vanilla extract
1/2 tsp. baking powder
dash salt
2/3 cup all purpose flour
1 cup chopped pecans

In medium bowl, stir by hand, the partialy melted butter and carob powder till smooth. Stir in sugar; add eggs and vanilla; mix till well blended. Stir in baking powder, salt and flour; add pecans. Spread batter into a well greased 8 inch square baking pan. Bake in 350 degree oven, 25-30 minutes, or till just set in center. (Don't overbake) Cool in pan; cut into 2 inch squares.
Yields 16 - 2 inch square brownies

Special Hint: If brownies are dry, shorten baking time about 5 minutes.

CAROB SWIRL BROWNIES

Sweet and rich; sure to please everyone

Preheat oven 350 degrees

1/4 cup butter or margarine
1 cup light brown sugar
1 egg
1 tsp. vanilla extract
3/4 cup whole wheat flour

1 tsp. baking powder
1/2 tsp. salt
1/2 cup **carob swirl filling,**
   recipe follows

Melt butter, cool. In medium bowl, stir melted butter and brown sugar together. Add egg and vanilla; beat to blend. With wooden spoon stir in flour, baking powder and salt till well mixed. Spread batter in well greased and floured 8 x 8 inch square baking pan. Prepare filling. Spoon filling over top of batter; carefully swirl filling into batter, being careful not to scrape bottom or side of pan. Bake in 350 degree oven 25-30 minutes. Center will be firm to touch. Cut into even squares. Cool.
Yields 16 squares

Carob swirl filling:

2 tblsp. butter or margarine,
   room temperature
1/4 cup carob powder

1/4 cup honey
2 tblsp. cream cheese, softened
3/4 tsp. vanilla extract

In small bowl, beat butter, carob powder and honey till smooth. Add cream cheese and vanilla; beat till smooth and creamy.
Variation: for carob nut swirl brownies, add 1/2 to 1 cup chopped nuts to batter after flour is mixed in.

FROSTED BROWNIES

Rich and sweet

Preheat oven 350 degrees

1/4 cup butter or margarine,
    room temperature
4 **carob oilbutter squares,**
    room temperature
2 eggs
3/4 cup sugar
1 tsp. vanilla extrat

3/4 cup flour
dash salt
1/2 tsp. baking powder
1/2 to 1 cup chopped nuts
fudge frosting & filling,
    (see section on frostings)

Beat together butter and carob squares till smooth. Add eggs, sugar and vanilla; mix well. Stir in flour, salt and baking powder to blend. Add nuts. Spread batter into well greased and floured 8 x 8 inch baking pan. Bake 350 degree oven 25-30 minutes. Cool in pan. Frost with small recipe fudge frosting & filling. Cut in 2 inch squares.
Yields 16 squares

Variation: for double carob frosted brownies add 3/4 cup carob chips when you add nuts.

EBONY BROWNIES

Moist brownies on top with a crunchy cookies crumb crust

Preheat oven 350 degrees

1 recipe **carob crumb crust**
    (see pie crust section)
2 eggs
4 **honey lite carob squares,**
    room temperature
1/3 cup all purpose flour

1/4 cup brown sugar
1/2 tsp. baking soda
1/4 cup melted butter or
    margarine, cooled
1 tsp. vanilla extract

Make **carob crumb crust;** press firmly into greased 8 x 8 inch square baking pan. Do not bake. Set aside. Using a food processor, place all remaining ingredients into processor container. Process a few seconds till mixture is smooth. Pour into prepared crust-lined baking pan; carefully spreading batter evenly to edges without scraping crust. Bake in 350 degree oven 30-35 minutes or till center tests done. Cool completely. Cut in 2 inch squares.
Yields 16 squares

Note: If brownies are not completely cooled before cutting, bottom crust will separate and crumble from top portion.

Variations:

▶

Two Toned Ebony Brownies: Use ebony brownie recipe, except use wafer crumb crust, (see pie crust section) instead of carob crumb crust.

Chip Filled Ebony Brownies: Make ebony brownie recipe, and add 1 cup carob chips to brownie batter *after* processing.

CAROB HONEY RUM BROWNIES

Cake brownies with a hint of rum! Add 1/2 to 1 cup chopped walnuts for a nutty variation.

Preheat oven 350 degrees

1/2 cup vegetable oil	1 tsp. baking soda
2 eggs	dash salt
3/4 cup honey	1 cup whole wheat flour
1 tsp. vanilla extract	1/2 cup carob powder
2 tblsp. dark rum	

1/2 Recipe:*

1/4 cup vegetable oil	1/2 tsp. baking soda
1 egg	dash salt
1/3 cup plus 1 tblsp. honey	1/2 cup whole wheat flour
1/2 tsp. vanilla extract	1/4 cup carob powder
1 tblsp. dark rum	

In medium mixing bowl, beat oil and eggs till smooth. Pour honey into mixture and beat. Add vanilla, rum, soda and salt. Stir in flour and carob powder. For main recipe — Pour batter into grease and flour 8 x 8 inch square pan. Bake on 350 degrees 25-30 minutes. Frost if desired. Cut into 2 inch squares.
Yields 16 squares

*Note: 1/2 recipe is used in special banana pudding in cheese cake section.

FUDGE TOPPED GOLDEN BROWNIES

A butterscotch brownie with fudge topping

Preheat oven 350 degrees

1/4 cup vegetable oil
1/2 cup brown sugar
1/4 cup molasses
1 large egg
3/4 cup whole wheat flour
1/2 tsp. baking powder

1/2 tsp. baking soda
1 tsp. vanilla extract
fudge frosting & filling, small
   recipe (see frosting section)
1/2 cup chopped pecans

Place all ingredients, except filling and pecans, in small bowl. Beat with electric mixer on low speed about 1 minute or till batter is smooth. Spread batter evenly into a well greased and floured 8 x 8 inch baking pan. Bake in 350 degree oven 20-25 minutes or till lightly browned and puffed; center will be set. Be careful not to over bake or edges will burn. Cool. Make Fudge Frosting & Filling. Stir pecans into frosting. Spread over cooled brownies evenly to cover. Cut in squares.   Yields 25 squares

ULTIMATE MINT BROWNIES

Just as the name implies

Preheat oven 375 degrees

Mint fudge filling, recipe follows
6 **carob oilbutter squares,**
   room temperature
3 eggs
1 cup brown sugar
1 tsp. vanilla extract

1 tsp. mint extract
1 tsp. baking soda
1 cup whole wheat flour
1/4 cup bran, optional
Mint flavored ice cream, optional

Prepare filling; chill overnight. In medium mixing bowl, beat carob squares, eggs, sugar and extracts till smooth and creamy. Blend in soda. Stir in flour, (and bran, if adding), till well mixed. Grease and flour two 8 x 8 inch square baking pans. Using 1/2 batter for each pan, divide batter equally and spread in each pan. Bake in 375 degree oven 15 to 20 minutes or till centers test done. Don't over bake. Leave in pans and let cool completely. When no longer warm, spread chilled filling over top of brownie in one pan. Carefully remove brownies from second pan and place over filling in 1st pan. Cover and refrigerate till serving. Cut in equal squares with sharp knife. Refrigerate. Serve on dessert plates and pass the ice cream!!
Yields 16 squares

Mint fudge filling:

1/4 cup canned, sweetened, condensed milk
4 **carobutter squares,** room temperature
1/3 cup butter, or margarine
1 cup sugar
1 tsp. vanilla extract
1 tsp. mint extract
8 ounces cream cheese

In small bowl, beat together canned milk and carob squares till smooth. In deep saucepan, combine butter, sugar and carob mixture. Stir together; heat on medium-low to melt butter and dissolve sugar.* Mixture will thicken and bubble. Stir easily, and continuously. When mixture reaches rolling boil, remove from heat immediately and let cool to 110 degrees (lukewarm) without stirring. When cooled, beat in vanilla, mint and cream cheese to thick, smooth consistency. Pour into bowl. Cover and refrigerate 4 hours or overnight.

*Note: Be patient when bringing carob mixture to rolling boil. Carob and milk will scorch if heat is on high setting.

Mint

MINTY CAROB CAKE W/PECANS recipe on page 55

CINNAMON CAROB TUNNEL CAKE recipe on page 56

3
CAKE

See Altitude Adjustment p. 8-9

FUDGEY CAROB CAKE

Preheat oven 350 degrees

1/3 cup milk
1 ounce vegetable oil
1/2 cup carob powder
1 egg
1 cup whole wheat pastry flour
1 cup all purpose flour
1 tsp. baking soda

2 tsp. baking powder
1/2 tsp. salt
1 tblsp. vanilla extract
2 eggs
3/4 cup honey
1/2 cup vegetable oil

In small bowl, place the milk, 1 ounce oil, carob powder and 1 egg. Mix together till smooth. Set aside. In medium bowl combine flours, soda, baking powder and salt. Stir dry ingredients together to combine. Set aside. In large mixing bowl beat on high speed, 2 eggs and vanilla. Add honey in a slow stream while beating. In a thin slow stream add the 1/2 cup oil, still beating on high. When mixture has thickened, turn speed down to low; add dry ingredients just to mix well. Still on low speed, add craob mixture. Beat till thoroughly mixed, about 1 more minute. Don't over beat. Pour into 2 well greased and floured 8 inch cake pans. Bake in preheated 350 degree oven 25-30 minutes. Top will start to crack and center will test done. Cool in pans 10-15 minutes, remove to racks to finish cooling. Frost with favorite frosting.
Yields 1 double layer 8 inch cake

Note: Be careful not to over bake carob desserts. They become very dry when over-baked.

53

MOCHA FUDGE CAKE

This cake really has a nice texture and tastes like cakes Mom use to make. Really!

Preheat oven 350 degrees

1 cup all purpose flour	1 & 3/4 tsp. baking soda
1/2 cup whole wheat flour	1 & 1/4 tsp. baking powder
1 & 1/2 cups sugar	3 eggs
1 cup carob powder	1/2 cup buttermilk
1/2 tsp. salt	2 tsp. vanilla extract
1/2 cup cold, strong, black coffee	1/2 cup vegetable oil

In large mixing bowl, combine flours, sugar, carob powder and salt; mix on low speed of electric mixer to thoroughly mix. Place coffee in a glass measure; stir in baking soda and baking powder, set aside. Make a well in center of dry ingredients in large bowl. Add eggs, buttermilk, vanilla, oil and coffee mixture. Beat on medium-high speed for 1 to 2 minutes. Pour into well greased and floured 9 x 13 inch cake pan, or two 8 inch round cake pans. Bake in 350 degree oven; 35 to 40 minutes -13 x 9 inch pan; 25 to 30 minutes - 8 inch round cake pans. Cool in pan. Frost with fudge mocha frosting (see frosting section).
Yields 1 - 9 x 13 inch oblong cake or 1 - 8 inch layer cake

CAROB GINGERCAKE

Take home 1st Prize with this delicious, spicy, carob flavored cake

Preheat oven 325 degrees

1 & 1/2 cups all purpose flour	1 & 1/2 tsp. ground cinnamon
1 & 1/4 cups whole wheat pastry flour	2 eggs
	1/2 cup honey
1 tsp. baking soda	1/2 cup molasses
1/2 tsp. salt	1 cup vegetable oil
2 tsp. baking powder	3/4 cup buttermilk
1 tsp. ground ginger	3 **lite carob squares,*** room temperature

Assemble ingredients. Combine flours, soda, salt, baking powder, ginger and cinnamon in a medium bowl, set aside. In large mixing bowl, place eggs; beat till lemony colored. Turn mixer speed to medium-high setting, add honey and molasses in a slow, fine stream, turning bowl steadily during mixing. When completely blended, turn to high speed and begin adding oil in slow steady stream, keeping bowl turning. As you add oil, mixture will become thickened and some what fluffy. (You have incorporated air into the mixture, which aids in leaving while cooking.) Lower mixer speed to medium setting. Adding flour mixture alternately with buttermilk, beginning with flour and ending with but-

▶

termilk. Work quickly, letting mixture beat smoothly until all flour mixture and buttermilk is added and mixture is smooth, about 2 minutes. Last add carob squares, beating in just till carob is blended into batter. Pour batter into 2 well greased and floured 8 inch round cake pans. Bake in 325 degree oven 30 to 40 minutes or till test done in center. Cool in pans 10 to 15 minutes. Turn out on cake racks to finish cooling.

Frost with fluffy vanilla cream frosting (see frosting section). Yields 1 double layer 8 inch cake

Helpful Hint: To substitute regular whole wheat flour for whole wheat pastry flour, place 2 to 3 cups w.w. flour into food processor container. Process for 1 to 2 minutes, then sift twice. Measure according to recipe specification.

*Note: Use 1/2 cup carob powder dissolved in 1/4 cup water instead of lite carob squares, if desired.

MINTY CAROB CAKE

Light, with the refreshing flavor of mint

Preheat oven 350 degrees

4 eggs	room temperature
1/2 cup vegetable oil	3/4 cup whole wheat flour
1/2 cup brown sugar	1 cup all purpose flour
1/2 cup honey	1 & 1/2 tsp. baking powder
1 & 1/2 tsp. mint extract	1/2 tsp. baking soda
1 tsp. vanilla extract	1/2 tsp. salt
2 **lite carob squares,**	1/4 cup buttermilk

In large mixing bowl beat eggs, oil and brown sugar in that order, till smooth, on high speed. Add honey slowly, by pouring in fine stream while continuing to beat on high. Mixture will slightly thicken. Turn speed down to medium; add extracts and carob squares; beat just to combine. Sift flours, baking powder, soda and salt together. Add dry mixture to carob mixture, add buttermilk; beat 1 minute. Pour into 2 well greased and floured 8 inch cake pans. Bake in preheat 350 degree oven 30-35 minutes. Cool in pans for 10 minutes. Remove from pans, cool on racks. Frost with minty carob frosting (see frosting section). Yields 1 8 inch layer cake

CINNAMON CAROB TUNNEL CAKE

A moist carob n' cinnamon center makes this bundt cake irresistible!

Preheat oven 350 degrees

1/2 cup vegetable oil	1 cup whole wheat flour
1/2 cup butter or margarine,	1/2 tsp. ground cinnamon
room temperature	3/4 tsp. baking soda
1 tsp. vanilla extract	1/2 tsp. baking powder
1 tsp. lemon extract	dash salt
1 & 2/3 cups sugar	1 cup buttermilk
3 eggs	1/2 cup raisins
1 & 1/2 cups all purpose flour	1 cup carob syrup, recipe follows

In large mixing bowl cream oil and butter till smooth. Blend in extracts, sugar and eggs beat till light. In separate bowl combine dry ingredients; stir dry mixture together to mix. Add 1/2 of dry mixture to the creamed mixture in mixing bowl; blending mixtures together while adding 1/2 buttermilk. Repeat with remaining dry ingredients and buttermilk. Beat 1 minute. Stir in raisins. Grease and flour 10 inch bundt pan. Remove 1 & 1/2 cups of batter, reserve. Pour remaining batter into prepared pan. Prepare Carob syrup. Add syrup to reserved batter; stir to mix. Carefully pour over cake batter in pan. Using a knife or handle of wooden spoon, slice through top of batter in center. Go around pan twice. Do not marble. Bake in 350 degree oven 55-65 minutes or till test done in center. Cool in pan 10-15 minutes. Remove to rack to cool. Drizzle with thin lemon icing or sprinkle top with powdered sugar. Yields 1   10 inch bundt cake

Carob Syrup:

1/2 cup carob powder	1/2 tsp. ground cinnamon
1/4 cup maple syrup	1/4 tsp. ground cloves
1/4 cup water	1/4 tsp. baking soda

Mix all ingredients together with fork till smooth.

QUICK RECIPES WITH BOX CAKES

CREAMY CAROB SWIRL CAKE

Preheat oven 325 degrees

1 18 ounce pkg. yellow cake mix
1 cup **creamy carob filling** (see frosting section)

Prepare cake mix as package instructs. Place cake batter in well greased and floured 12 cup bundt pan. Spoon carob filling over top of batter with large spoons full. Gently swirl filling into cake batter, being careful not to touch

sides or bottom of cake pan with spoon. Bake on 325 degrees for 45 to 55 minutes, or till tests done. Cool in pan 10 to 15 minutes. Turn out on cake racks to finish cooling. Sprinkle with powdered sugar if desired. or sweet powder (see frosting section).
Yields 1 12 inch bundt cake

ANGEL FOOD CAKE WITH BITTERSWEET CAROB SAUCE

Preheat oven as directed on package

Prepare and cook cake as directed. Cool cake; Pour bittersweet carob sauce (see frosting section) over top. Serve.

CAROB FILLED BOSTON CREAM PIE

Preheat oven as directed on package

Prepare cake as directed. When preparing filling, at end of mixing, beat in 2 carobutter squares, room temp. continue preparing as directed. If desire, for glaze, use creamy carob orange glaze (see frosting section).

CAROB CAKE FROM MIX

Preheat oven as directed on package

1 yellow or white package cake mix (standard size)
2-4 carob baking square, your choice, room temp.

Beat carob squares in when adding oil, shortening or butter, depending on which one package calls for.

ZUCCHINI CAROB BUNDT CAKE

Now a days, just about everyone has their own version of this favorite — here is mine, soon to be yours!

Preheat oven 350 degrees

1 cup whole wheat flour	room temperature
1 & 1/2 cups all purpose flour	1/2 cup vegetable oil
1/2 cup carob powder	1 tblsp. vanilla extract
1/2 cup dry powdered milk	1 & 1/2 cups sugar
2 tsp. baking soda	3 eggs
1/2 tsp. cream of tartar	2 cups finely grated zucchini
1/2 tsp. salt	1/2 cup buttermilk
1 tsp. cinnamon	1 cup chopped nuts
1/4 cup butter or margarine,	

Combine first 8 (dry) ingredients into a bowl, stir, set aside. In large mixing

▶

bowl, beat butter, oil, vanilla and sugar on high speed, till thick carmel colored. Turn mixer speed down to medium; add eggs, one at a time, beat just till mixed in. Turn speed down to low; add zucchini. Continue beating on low; add buttermilk alternately with dry ingredients, ending with buttermilk. Beat thoroughly; about 1 minute. Don't over beat. Stir in chopped nuts. Pour batter into well greased and floured 10 inch bundt pan. Bake in 350 degree oven 45-50 minutes or till top cracks and center tests done. Cool 10-15 minutes in pan. Remove to rack to finish cooling. Frost with favorite cream cheese frosting.
Yields 1   10 inch bundt cake

CAROB CHERRY-SAUCE CAKE

Moist and light textured with a delicate flavor of cherries from the cherry applesauce

Preheat oven 350 degrees

5 **caroboil squares,**	2 tsp. baking soda
room temperature	dash salt
3/4 cup brown sugar	1 & 1/4 cup all purpose
3 eggs	flour, sifted
1 tsp. almond extract	1 cup whole wheat flour, sifted
1/2 tsp. vanilla extract	1 & 1/2 cups cherry applesauce*

Beat caroboil squares, brown sugar and eggs together on medium high speed about 2 minutes. Add extracts, baking soda and salt; beat in. Sift flours together. Add flours alternately with cherry applesauce, ending with cherry applesauce. On medium speed beat 1 minute longer, scraping sides of bowl.

Grease and flour 13 x 9 x 2 inch baking pan. Spread batter evenly into prepared pan. Bake 350 degrees for 30-35 minutes or till center test done. Cool completely.

Sprinkle cooled cake with powdered sugar or sweet powder (see frosting section). Serve with additional cherry applesauce if desired. Yields a 13 x 9 inch cake.

***Variations:** Cherry applesauce is just one of the fruit combinations with applesauce. Others are peach, apricot and strawberry. Try substituting any of the fruit variations. You will find them in your grocery store with the applesauce.

CAROB LANE CAKE

3 thin cake layers, filled with a date-raisin carob filling

Preheat oven 350 degrees

7 eggs, separated
1/2 tsp. cream of tartar
1/3 cup sugar
1 & 3/4 cups sifted all
    purpose flour
2 tsp. baking powder
1/2 tsp. baking soda
1/2 tsp. salt
3/4 cup sugar

3/4 cup water
5 **sweet caroboil squares,**
    room temperature
Date-raisin carob filling,
    recipe below
1 cup chopped pecans
sour cream icing (see
    frosting section)
Whole pecans for garnish

Separate eggs, reserve 2 of egg yolks for filling. Place egg whites in a large mixing bowl. Beat on high speed with cream of tartar, till frothy. Slowly add the 1/3 cup sugar; beating till stiff peaks form. (Don't beat dry) Set aside. In small bowl, combine flour, baking powder, soda, salt and 3/4 cup sugar. Stir dry ingredients to thoroughly mix. In another bowl, beat together water, carob squares and 5 of egg yolks. Blend in dry mixture till thick and well mixed, about 1 minute. Using wire whisk, gently fold beaten egg whites into carob mixture. Turning whisk easily through mixture to form a light - airy batter; being careful not to over-mix. Grease bottom of 9 x 13 inch pan. Line bottom of pan with 9 x 13 inch piece of wax paper. Lightly grease top of wax paper. Pour 1/3 of batter into prepared pan, spreading evenly to edges of pan. Bake in 350 degree oven 15-20 minutes. Cool in pan for 15 minutes. Loosen edges carefully from pan with knife. Place a cooling rack, same size as pan over top of pan. Invert cake onto rack, gently, using wax paper to hold cake together. When cake is free from pan, peel wax paper from cake. Repeat 2 more times with remaining cake batter, (making 3 layers). Prepare filling. Place 1st cake onto oblong cake platter. Using 1/2 of filling, spoon evenly over top of cake, spreading over surface. Sprinkle with 1/2 cup of chopped pecans. Place 2nd cake layer over top. Spread with remaining filling, sprinkle remaining pecans over filling. Top with 3rd layer. Ice with sour cream icing; garnish with whole pecans.

Date-raisin carob filling:

2 egg yolks, reserved
1/3 cup butter
1/2 cup honey
1 tsp. vanilla extract
3 **honey caroboil squares,**

    room temperature
1 & 1/2 cup finely
    chopped dates
1 cup chopped raisins

Place egg yolks, butter and honey in saucepan. Stir on low heat till mixture thickens. Remove heat; cool 5 minutes. Stir in carob squares and vanilla. Mix well. Add dates and raisins.

UPSIDE-DOWN APPLESAUCE CAKE

Applesauce topping cooks under batter, so when cake is turned out onto serving plate — it has instant topping!!

Preheat oven 350 degrees

Cake batter:

1/4 cup vegetable oil
1/2 cup sugar
2 eggs
1/2 tsp. vanilla extract
1/2 tsp. orange extract
1/4 cup carob powder

1 cup all purpose flour
1 tsp. baking soda
3/4 tsp. baking powder
dash salt
1 tsp. cinnamon
3/4 cup applesauce

Applesauce topping:

1/3 cup melted butter
  or margarine
1/2 cup brown sugar

1 tsp. cinnamon
1/2 cup applesauce

In medium mixing bowl combine vegetable oil, sugar, eggs, extracts and carob powder. Beat on medium speed till well blended. Turn mixer speed down; beat in flour, soda, baking powder, salt, cinnamon and applesauce. Beat one more minute. Set batter aside. In small bowl mix together all of topping ingredients. Pour topping ingredients into 8 inch square baking dish; spread evenly over bottom. Carefully pour cake batter over top, making sure not to mix two mixtures together. Bake in 350 degree oven 25-30 minutes or till center springs back at touch. Cool for 10 minutes. Loosen cake edges with sharp knife. Turn out onto serving plate. Spoon any topping left in baking dish on to cake. Cut into squares. Serve with vanilla ice cream. Refrigerate any leftovers.
Yields single layer 8 inch square cake.

Variations: Upside-Down Appplesauce N' Walnut Cake — Add 1 cup of chopped walnuts to topping mixture before pouring cake batter over top.

Upside-Down Fudge Applesauce Cake — Beat 1 lite carob square, room temperature, into topping mixture, omit cinnamon; add 1 tsp. vanilla extract.

CAROB BRAN SPICE CAKES

These little cakes are as light as a feather

Preheat oven 350 degrees

1 cup all purpose flour
1/2 cup bran, raw
1 tsp. baking soda

1 tsp. cinnamon, ground
1 egg
1/4 cup honey

►

1/4 cup carob powder	1/4 cup molasses
1/2 tsp. salt	1/2 cup vegetable oil
1 tsp. ginger, ground	1/2 cup sour cream

Sift dry ingredients together. In medium mixing bowl cream egg, honey and molasses. Beating on high speed, slowly add oil in fine stream. Mixture will thicken. Turn mixer down to medium speed, add dry mixture alternately with sour cream. Beat just till well mixed. Grease and flour 2 inch muffin cups. Fill 1/2 to 2/3 full. Bake in 350 degree oven 20 to 25 minutes. Let cool in pan about 10 minutes. Loosen edges with knife and finish cooling on racks. Drizzle with cream cheese icing (see frosting section)
Yields 12   2 inch cup cakes.

CAROB HOLIDAY CAKE

Full of nuts, cherries and raisins, this cake makes a delicious version of holiday fruitcake.

Baking temperature 350 degrees

1 pkg. baking yeast	3 eggs
1/4 cup warm water	2 tsp. vanilla extract
1 tblsp. honey	1/2 cup carob powder
1 cup warm milk	1/2 tsp. salt
2 cups all purpose flour	1 tsp. soda
1 cup whole wheat flour	1 cup raisins
1/2 cup melted butter,	2 cups coarsley
cool to warm	chopped pecans
1/4 cup vegetable oil	2 cups chopped, drained
1 cup honey	maracshino cherries

Sprinkle yeast over warm water; let stand 5 minutes. Stir the 1 tablespoon honey into dissolved yeast. In large mixing bowl beat together on low speed warm milk, 1 cup of all purpose flour and whole wheat flour. Mixture will be thick. Add yeast mixture, butter, oil, honey, eggs, vanilla and carob powder. Continue to beat 2 minutes on medium speed. Add remaining 1 cup all purpose flour, salt and soda; beat in. Let batter stand 45 minutes. Batter will rise slightly. Beat batter down. Pour into well greased 12 cup bundt pan or 3 well greased 8 x 4 inch loaf pans. Let rise about 2-3 hours or till almost doubled. Bake in preheated 350 degree oven. Bundt pan 40-60 minutes; loaf pans 35-45 minutes, or till tests done. Cool 35 minutes in pans. Remove to racks to finish cooling. When completely cooled wrap tightly and store in refrigerator or freezer for 2 weeks if desired.
Yields 1 bundt cake or 3 loaves.

Note: Rising time may vary according to kitchen temperatures. A warm kitchen will take less time for batter to rise. A cool kitchen may take longer.

SILK FUDGE FROSTING recipe on page 64

4
FROSTING & FILLING

FUDGE FROSTING* & FILLING

Makes a beautiful and traditional type frosting using less powdered sugar

Large Recipe:

2 **sweet carobutter squares,**
    room temperature
2 **sweet lite carob squares,**
    room temperature

1 tsp. vanilla extract
8 ounces cream cheese,
    room temperature
2 cups powdered sugar

In medium bowl, mix together all ingredients and beat till smooth and velvety. Yields 1 & 3/4 cups

Small Recipe:

1 **sweet carobutter square,**
    room temperature
1 **sweet lite carob square,**
    room temperature

1/2 tsp. vanilla extract
4 ounces cream cheese,
    room temperature
1 cup powdered sugar

In small bowl, beat together all ingredients till smooth and velvety. Yields about 3/4 cup

*Fudge Mocha Frosting: Make above recipe; add 1 tblsp. mocha flavoring to large recipe or 1 & 1/2 tsp. to small recipe.

FLUFFY VANILLA CREAM FROSTING

This frosting needs refrigerating before frosting cake, so start preparing it while the cake cooks.

12 ounces cream cheese,
   room temperature
1/3 cup honey

1 & 1/2 tsp. vanilla extract
3 tblsp. soft butter,
   not melted

Beat cream cheese and butter till smooth. Add honey and vanilla; beat on high speed of electric mixer about 1 minute till smooth. Cover and chill for 1 hour. Yields 2 cups

Frost completely cooled cake. To store: cover loosely and place in refrigerator.

SILK FUDGE FROSTING

Creamy and delicately sweet

2 & 1/2 cups powder sugar
1 cup carob powder
1/4 cup, softened butter
1 cup cream cheese,

   room temperature
2 tsp. almond extract
1 tsp. vanilla extract

Combine all ingredients in small bowl. Mix or beat till smooth, satiny, spreading consistency.
Yeilds 2 cups

CAROB BUTTER FROSTING

Rich buttery frosting that is not overly sweet*

1/2 cup soft butter
4 **sweet carobutter squares,**
   room temperature

1 cup powdered sugar
1/2 tsp. vanilla extract
1/2 tsp. almond extract

Mix all ingredients in medium bowl; beat together till creamy smooth consistency.   Yields 1 & 1/4 to 1 & 1/2 cups

*Note: You may add 1/2 to 1 cup additional powdered sugar if this frosting is not sweet enough for your taste.

BUTTER CREAM CAROB FROSTING

Silky texture — lightly sweetened*

1/2 cup butter,
   room temperature
4 **carob cream squares,**
   room temperature

1 & 1/2 cups powdered sugar
1/2 tsp. vanilla extract

In medium bowl, beat all ingredients till light and fluffy. Frost completely cooled cake.

*Note: Add about 1/2 to 1 cup additional powdered sugar if sweeter frosting is desired.

SEMI-SWEET CREAMY CAROB FROSTING

Healthier than most frostings

6 **carob cream squares,**
   room temperature

1/3 cup honey
1 tblsp. vanilla extract

Place all ingredients in small bowl; stir together with fork till creamy, smooth, spreading consistency.
Yields about 1 cup.

Half Recipe

3 **carob cream squares,**
   room temperature

1 & 1/2 tsp. vanilla extract
3 tbls. honey

Follow recipe instructions above.   Yields 1/2 cup

SOUR CREAM CAROBUTTER FROSTING

A traditional frosting

4 **carobutter squares,**
   room temperature
1/2 cup sour cream

2 tsp. vanilla extract
3 cups powdered sugar

Beat carobutter squares, sour cream and vanilla in a medium bowl to thick creamy mixture. Stir in powdered sugar till smooth, spreading consistency.
Yields 1 & 1/2 cups

MINTY CAROB FROSTING

Honey and mint — refreshing combination

4 **honey carobutter squares,**
    room temperature
4 ounces cream cheese,
    room temperature

1/4 cup butter,
    room temperature
1 tsp. mint extract*
1/3 cup honey

Place all ingredients in small bowl and beat till light and creamy. Frosts a double layer cake.   Yields 1 & 1/2 to 1 & 2/3 cups

*Note: If you substitute peppermint extract for mint extract, decrease measure to 1/2 tsp. as peppermint is a much stronger flavor.

Variation: Omit mint extract. Replace with vanilla; almond; cherry or orange extract.

CREAM CHEESE ICING

6 ounces cream cheese, room temperature
1/2 cup honey
1 tsp. orange extract

Combine all ingredients; beat till smooth. Drizzle over cake or cookies.
Yields about 1 & 1/4 cups

Variation: Substitute any desired flavor extract for the orange extract for a taste change.

SOUR CREAM ICING

2 tblsp. softened
    cream cheese
1/2 cup sour cream

1 tsp. vanilla extract
1 & 1/2 cups **sweet powder,**
    recipe following

Beat cream cheese, sour cream and vanilla till smooth. Beat in sweet powder till the consistency of thin icing. Drizzle over cakes or cookies.
Yields about 2/3 cup

SWEET POWDER

This powder can be used instead of pure powdered sugar in lots of recipes. You can sprinkle it over cakes, cookies, sweet rolls; or mix it in place of pure powdered sugar in your favorite frostings and icings. It's not as sweet, but has a creamy rich taste and less calories

2 cups powdered milk
2 cups powdered sugar

Place both ingredients in a food processor container; cover and process to fine powder. Store in a sealed container in pantry or cabinet.

To make vanilla favored sweet powder, place a whole vanilla bean in container with powder. Before measuring powder for recipe, remove the vanilla bean then replace it when finished measuring.

BITTERSWEET CAROB SAUCE

Can be used as an icing on cakes, sauce for ice cream or not too sweet, but rich topping for a number of desserts

1/2 cup carob powder
2 slightly rounded
   tblsp. cornstarch
1/2 cup honey

3/4 cup water
1 tblsp. butter
1 & 1/2 tsp. vanilla extract

In small saucepan combine carob powder, cornstarch, honey and water. Stir with wire whisk to dissolve the dry ingredients. Place over medium heat, stirring constantly, till sauce is thick and rich; about 5 minutes. Remove from heat; add butter and vanilla. Sauce will be velvety.
Yields about 1 & 1/3 cups.

CREAMY CAROB ORANGE GLAZE

Mildly sweet with the flavor of carob enhanced with orange

4 **carob cream squares,**
   room temperature

1/4 cup honey
1 tsp. orange extract

In small bowl, stir together all ingredients till very smooth.
Yields about 3/4 cup

CREAMY CAROB FILLING

This filling is used in several recipes. It can be baked in some recipes; or used as filling after baking.

1/2 cup butter or margarine,
    room temperature
1 cup carob powder

1 cup honey
1/2 cup cream cheese
1 tblsp. vanilla extract

Beat butter, carob powder and honey till smooth. Add cream cheese and vanilla; beat till creamy. Yields 2 cups

Use chart below for adjusting measurements for different recipe selections.

Adjusted measure chart:

YIELDS —	2 CUPS	1 & 1/2 CUPS	1 CUP	1/2 CUP
Butter	1/2 cup	1/3 cup	1/4 cup	2 tblsp.
Carob Pwd.	1 cup	3/4 cup	1/2 cup	1/4 cup
Honey	1 cup	3/4 cup	1/2 cup	1/4 cup
Crm. cheese	1/2 cup	1/3 cup	1/4 cup	2 tblsp.
Van. Ext.	1 tblsp.	2 & 1/4 tsp.	1 & 1/2 tsp.	3/4 tsp.

PEPPERMINT FILLING

A refreshing center filling for cookies or cakes

1/3 cup butter,
    softened, not melted

2/3 cup powdered sugar
1/4 tsp. peppermint extract

In small bowl, beat all ingredients together till light and fluffy. Yields 1/3 to 1/2 cup.

ALMOND BUTTER CREAM

Creamy, smooth — and easy to make

2 ounces almond bark
1 Tblsp. butter,
   room temperature

4 ounces cream
   cheese, room temperature

In small bowl, melt almond bark in microwave, about 2 minutes, till creamy. Add soft butter and cream cheese. Stir till smooth and completely blended.
   Yields 3/4 cup

ALMOND CAROB CARAMEL FILLING

A cooked fudge-like filling

1 small can evaporated
   milk, (5 & 1/2 ounces)
1/4 cup butter
1/2 cup plus 2 tblsp. honey
3 ounces almond bark

4 carob cream squares,
   room temperature
1 cup lightly toasted,
   chopped almonds

In medium saucepan, combine evaporated milk, butter and honey. Heat on medium-low heat, stirring constantly, to melt butter. When mixture begins to bubble and thicken, it will turn dark caramely colored. Continue stirring and cook till candy thermometer reads 234 degrees; (soft ball stage). Remove from heat; stir in almond bark. Stir till melted. Add carob squares; mix to dissolve. Beat with electric mixer till smooth and dark. Stir in chopped almonds. Use warm, to frost cookies, or place in covered bowl and chill for thicker consistency. Frost a 13 x 9 inch cake; or use as filling for cookies or tarts.
Yields about 2 & 1/2 cups

OL' FASHIONED FUDGE recipe on page 71

5

CANDY

Homemade candy is special to everyone and can always bring back fond memories of other times. Carob can be a delightful addition to your special candy recipes. Here are some pleasing fudge and confection recipes for those special occasions when you want someone to think back to fond memories of your candy and home.

OL' FASHIONED FUDGE

2 & 1/3 cups sugar
1 small can (5.33 ounces)
    evaporated milk
2 tblsp. corn syrup

2 tsp. vanilla extract
4 **carobutter squares,**
    room temperature
1 cup chopped pecans

Prepare 8 x 8 inch square dish. See special note for preparing candy dishes. Butter inside of deep saucepan. Place sugar, milk and corn syrup in sauce pan. Stir together to mix. Cook over medium heat, stirring slowly and constantly, to dissolve sugar. Cook to 234 degrees on candy thermometer, (soft ball stage). Immediately remove from heat; place vanilla and carob squares on top of mixture without stirring. Let mixture cool down to 110 degrees, (lukewarm). When cooled, beat carob squares and vanilla into mixture till thick and smooth. (Don't over beat) Quickly stir in nuts and pour into prepared dish. Let fudge stand till set. With sharp knife, cut into 1 & 1/2 inch squares.
Yields about 3 dozen pieces

Mint Fudge Variation: Make "Ol' Fashioned Fudge", add 1 & 1/2 tsp. mint extract when adding vanilla.

Special Note: To prepare candy dish, butter appropriate size dish very well. Cut a piece of wax paper the same size as dish. Place on bottom of dish. Butter wax paper. Spoon or pour fudge into prepared dish. To remove each cut piece, gently loosen fudge from sides of dish, carefully slide thin metal spatula or small fork under each piece and lift out. To remove entire piece, carefully invert dish onto serving plate, sliding candy onto plate; peel wax paper from bottom.

PEANUT BUTTER N' CAROB FUDGE

2 cups sugar
2/3 cup milk, scalded, cooled
2 tblsp. corn syrup
2 tsp. vanilla extract

4 **sweet carob oilbutter squares,**
    room temperature
1/2 cup smooth peanut butter

Prepare a 9 x 5 inch dish. See special note for preparing candy dish, p. 71. Set aside. Butter inside of deep saucepan. Place sugar, milk and corn syrup in saucepan. Stir to mix. Cook over low heat, stirring slowly and constantly, till sugar is dissolved. Turn heat up to medium heat; cook to 234 degrees on candy thermometer, (soft ball stage). Immediately remove from heat; add vanilla, carob squares and peanut butter *but do not stir.* Let stand till candy is 110 degrees, (lukewarm). When cooled, beat till thick and smooth; about 2 minutes. Mixture will thicken and still be smooth. Don't over beat. Working quickly, spoon into prepared dish. Let stand to set candy. Cut in 1 inch squares.
Yields about 3 dozen pieces

NO COOK FUDGE

8 ounces cream cheese,
    room temperature
1/4 cup butter,
    room temperature

4 cups powdered sugar
3/4 carob powder
2 tsp. vanilla extract
1 cup chopped pecans or walnuts

In medium bowl, beat together, by hand, cream cheese, butter, powdered sugar, carob powder and vanilla till creamy and well blended. Stir in nuts. Spoon into prepared 8 x 8 inch dish. See special note for preparing candy dish, p. 71. Cut into even squares. Cover, Chill.
Yields about 2 & 1/2 dozen pieces

Variations:
Cherry Surprise Fudge: Make "No Cook Fudge", omit nuts. After fudge has been spooned into 8 x 8 inch dish, press 32 well drained, whole maraschino cherries evenly into fudge, about 1 inch apart, so each square of fudge will have cherry center.

Minty No Cook Fudge: Make "No Cook Fudge", omit nuts and add 1 & 1/2 tsp. mint extract when adding vanilla.

Special Hint: Humidity can cause candy to hold too much moisture. Use more powdered sugar if nessasary on humid days.

CASTLEBERRY PIE

Serve warm with ice cream or serve it cold with whip cream

Preheat oven 375 degrees

1 - 9 inch **easy frozen**
  carob crust, unbaked
  (see index)
1/2 cup frozen raspberry juice
  concentrate, undiluted
1/4 cup sugar*

1/4 cup cornstarch or 1/3 cup flour
16 ounces frozen strawberries, thawed
12 ounces frozen raspberries, thawed
3 tblsp. butter or margarine
Fresh strawberries for garnish
Vanilla Ice Cream or Whip Cream

Place undiluted juice concentrate in medium saucepan. Stir in sugar and corn-starch (or flour). Stir till cornstarch is completely dissolved. Place on medium-high heat. Stirring constantly till mixture thickens and begins to bubble. Cook 1 minute longer, continue to stir. Remove from heat; add thawed berries. Stir to coat berries with fruit sauce. Pour into prepared crust. Dot with butter evenly over top. Bake in 375 degree oven for 45 to 60 minutes, or till fruit is set in center. Garnish with whole fresh strawberries. Sprinkle with powdered sugar, if desired. Serve warm with ice cream or serve cold with whip cream. Serves 8 Yields 1 - 9 inch pie

*Note: for the real sweet lovers, add 1/4 cup additional sugar when adding sugar.

CASTLEBERRY PIE recipe above

FUDGE FILLED CHIFFON PIE

This pie is rich yet has a lightness that makes it a perfect dessert after any meal.

Preheat oven 375 degrees

wafer crumb crust
(see index)
8 **honey carob oilbutter**
squares, room temperature
1 & 1/2 cup milk
1 envelope unflavored gelatin

1/2 cup honey
2 eggs, separated
1 tblsp. butter
2 tsp. vanilla extract
1/8 tsp. cream of tartar
1 tblsp. sugar

Prepare crumb crust and cool completely. When cooled, spread the carob squares evenly over bottom and slightly up sides of crust. Place in refrigerator to chill while preparing chiffon.

Place milk into a medium bowl, sprinkle the gelatin over top. Let stand for 5 minutes. Stir, then add the honey and egg yolks, beat till blended. Place in medium saucepan and cook on medium-low heat, stirring constantly, till mixture just starts to bubble and slightly thickens. Remove from heat and stir in 1 tblsp. butter and vanilla. Pour into small bowl and chill till mixture mounds on spoon. Will take 2 - 3 hours, stir mixture occasionally while chilling.

Place egg whites in medium bowl, beat till frothy. Add cream of tartar and beat to soft peaks, add the 1 tblsp. sugar and beat to stiff peaks. Gently fold meringue into thickened chilled mixture. Pour over carob coated crust and spread evenly over top. Chill for about 3 hours.   Yields 1 - 9 inch pie

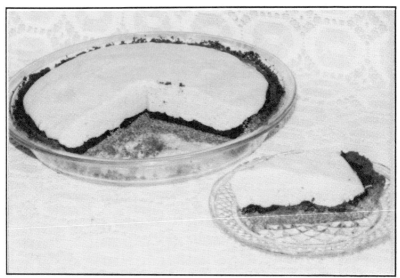

FUDGE FILLED CHIFFON PIE recipe above

CAROB CREAM PIE

A delicious version of an old favorite!!

Preheat oven 375 degrees

1 - 9 inch baked and 　cooled pastry shell	2 tblsp. butter
1/2 cup sugar	2 tsp. vanilla extract
1/3 cup flour	1/2 cup carob syrup,
dash salt	(1/3 cup carob powder and
1/4 cup powdered milk	1/3 cup water beat together
1 & 1/2 cups milk	till smooth)
3 egg yolks, lightly beaten	Meringue, below

Prepare filling:

In saucepan mix together sugar, flour, salt and powdered milk. Gradually stir in the milk to dissolve dry ingredients to make smooth, lump free mixture. Place over medium heat; stir constantly with wire whisk till mixture thickens. Remove from heat. Stir 3 tablespoon of hot mixture into beaten yolks, rapidly. Stir back into hot mixture, stirring quickly. Return mixture to heat. Cook just till mixture thickens to pudding consistency, stirring constantly. Remove from heat and turn burner off. Still using wire whisk, add butter, vanilla and carob syrup. Whisk till smooth and creamy. Pour into prepared pastry shell. Top with meringue.

Meringue:

3 eggs whites	1/3 cup sugar
1/4 tsp. cream of tartar	1 tsp. vanilla extract

Beat egg whites in large mixing bowl, on high speed, till frothy. Add cream of tartar, beat in. Gradually add sugar, beating to stiff peaks. Beat in vanilla.

Spread meringue over carob filling in shell. Seal meringue to edges of crust. Bake 375 degrees 10 minutes or till lightly browned. Let pie stand about 1 hour before serving.　　Yields 1 - 9 inch pie

Note: Add 1 tblsp. cocoa powder to carob syrup if desired.

LITE CAROB PECAN PIE

Flavorful pie with a light texture and easy to make

Preheat oven 350 degrees

4 eggs	(or dark corn syrup)
1/3 cup carob powder	1 tblsp. vanilla extract
1/4 cup melted butter, cooled	1 tblsp. cornstarch
1/2 cup honey	1 - 9 inch unbaked pie crust
1/4 cup molasses,	1 cup whole or chopped pecans

In a food processor container combine all of ingredients except pie crust and pecans. Process till thoroughly mixed, about 30 to 40 seconds. Sprinkle 1 tblsp. sugar over bottom of unbaked crust. Place pecans evenly over top. Carefully pour egg-honey mixture over pecans. Bake in 350 degree oven 45 to 55 minutes or till center is softly set. Cool completely. Serve with vanilla ice cream.
Yields 1 - 9 inch pie

CAROB CHERRY REFRIGERATOR PIE

A creamy jelled pie with the subtle flavor of cherries

1 baked 8 inch pie	2 tsp. cherry extract
shell, cooled	3 **carobutter squares,**
1 envelope unflavored	room temperature
gelatin, (1 Tblsp.)	1 tsp. vanilla extract
1 & 1/4 cups milk	1/8 tsp. cream of tartar
1/2 cup honey	4 tblsp. sugar
2 eggs, separated	whipped cream garnish
1 tsp. vanilla extract	maraschino cherries, garnish

Sprinkle gelatin over cold milk; let stand 5 minutes. In saucepan combine the milk-gelatin mixture, honey and 2 eggs yolks. Stirring constantly cook on medium heat about 5-7 minutes to dissolve gelatin. Mixture will just begin to bubble and coat spoon. Remove from heat. Let stand one minute. Stir in vanilla and cherry extract and carob squares. Cool for 10 minutes. Pour into bowl, cover and chill till mixture mounds slightly but not jelled.

Beat the 2 egg whites until frothy; add vanilla and cream of tartar. Beat in sugar, 1 tablespoon at a time. Beat till stiff peaks form. Fold into thickened, carob mixture. Pour into prepared crust. Chill thoroughly. Top with whip cream and maraschino cherries.
Yields 1 - 8 inch pie

Helpful Tip: If a sweeter pie is desired, use honey carobutter squares in place of carobutter squares.

MANDARIN ORANGE MERINGUE PIE

Mandarin orange segments in the filling and a ginger spice crust give a great flavor variation in this version of an old favorite.

Preheat oven 375 degrees

1 prepare 10 inch **carob ginger snap crust** (see index)
1 - 16 ounce can mandarin orange segments in light syrup
1/4 cup cornstarch
1 cup sugar

4 large eggs, separated
1 tblsp. butter
1 tblsp. grated orange rind
2 tsp. orange extract
Meringue, below

Drain juice from mandarin orange segments for 1 hour, reserve orange segments. Be sure to drain canned fruit well or you risk having your crust get a little soggy around the edges. Juice will equal about 3/4 cup; add enough water to equal 1 & 3/4 cups. Place cornstarch and sugar in medium saucepan and stir to mix. Add the juice-water mixture and stir. Place on medium-high heat stirring constantly with wire whisk till mixture boils; cook 1 more minute. Remove 1/4 cup of hot mixture and stir into slightly beaten egg yolks, return mixture to hot mixture in saucepan and stir in quickly. Turn heat down to low and continue stirring; cook for 2 minutes longer. Mixture will be thick, with a rich yellow color. Remove from heat, add butter, grated peel, and extract; stir in. Gently fold in reserved orange segments. Pour into prepared Carob Ginger Snap Crust. Top with meringue. Bake in 375 degree oven for 10-15 minutes, till meringue is lightly browned.   Yields 1 - 10 inch pie

Meringue:

4 egg whites, reserved
1/4 tsp. cream of tartar

1 tblsp. sugar
1 tsp. vanilla extract

In large bowl beat egg whites on high speed till foamy; add cream of tartar. Beat in sugar and vanilla till still peaks form. Spread evenly over pie filling, sealing at crust.

Pineapple Meringue Pie Variation: Substitute 1 - 16 ounce can crushed pineapple, (unsweetened), for mandarine orange segments. Drain and follow same procedure as above.

CAROB ANGLE PIE

Make meringue shell ahead, so it can cool. This pie is an elegant dessert, and should be served same day as made.

1 large pkg. instant vanilla pudding mix, (6 serving size)
3 **carob cream squares,** room temperature
Almond Meringue Shell or Tarts, recipes follow

Prepare pudding according to package directions. Beat in carob squares till creamy smooth. Fill prepared and cooled shell or divide pudding evenly into 6 tarts.   Yields 1 - 9 inch pie or 6 tarts

Almond Meringue Shell:

Preheat oven 200 degrees

3 egg whites   1/2 cup plus 2 tblsp. sugar
1/8 tsp. cream of tartar   1/2 tsp. almond extract

In large mixing bowl beat egg whites on high speed, till foamy; add cream of tartar and beat to soft peaks. Beat in salt and extract. Continuing to beat on high speed, add the sugar - 1 tablespoon at a time; beating to stiff, glossy peaks. Spoon meringue into greased 9 inch pie pan; spread evenly over bottom and up sides of dish, to form shell. Bake in 200 degree oven for 1 hour and 45 minutes; shell will be lightly browned; don't open the oven door, turn temperature off and leave in oven for 1 to 1 & 1/2 hours longer. Remove from oven and cool longer if shell is still warm. Fill with carob pudding.

Meringue Tart Shells:

Preheat oven 200 degrees

Make meringue shell recipe above, using vanilla extract in place of almond extract if desired. Lightly grease 6 small 5 inch tart pans. Using 1/2 to 3/4 cup of meringue for each tart pan spread evenly into shell shape. Bake in 200 degree oven 1 hour and 15 minutes or till delicately browned. Don't open oven door. Turn off and leave in oven for about 45 minutes longer. Remove from oven and let cool completely. Fill with carob pudding.

SWEET ALMOND FUDGE FILLED MERINGUES

Sweet and sinfully delicious

Preheat oven 375 degrees

1 recipe **meringue tart shells, prepared** (see above recipe)
1 recipe **almond carob caramel filling** (see frosting section)

▶

Meringue Topping:

3 eggs whites	1/3 cup sugar
1/4 tsp. cream of tartar	1 tsp. vanilla extract

Beat egg whites in large mixing bowl, on high speed, till frothy. Add cream of tartar, beat in. Gradually add sugar, beating to stiff peaks. Beat in vanilla.

Prepare meringue tart shells as directed, let dry in oven. Prepare almond carob caramel filling. Spread 1/4 to 1/3 cup filling over bottom and sides of prepared meringues. Prepare meringue topping. Spread topping over top of fudge filled meringue tarts, dividing topping equally on 6 tarts. Brown meringue in preheated 375 degree oven about 7 - 10 minutes or till delicately browned. Serve immediately.   Yields 6 meringue tarts

CAROB CRUMB CRUST

Preheat oven 325 degrees (for prebaked crust)

30 vanilla wafer	1/4 cup carob powder
1/2 cup walnuts	7 tblsp. cold butter

Break wafers in pieces and place in food processor container with walnuts and carob powder. Process till fine crumbs - a few seconds. Cut butter into 1/2 inch cubes. Place butter cubes into food processor container with crumbs; distribute evenly through crumb mixture. Cover and process about 20-30 seconds to make fine crumbs. Press into 9 or 10 inch pie pan or spring form pan. For prebake crust bake in a slow 325 degree oven 15-20 minutes, checking periodically to keep from over browning. Cool.
Yields 1 - 9 or 10 inch pie crust

CAROB GINGER SNAP CRUST

Preheat oven 400 degrees

30 - 2 inch ginger snap cookies, crushed to equal 2 cups	2 tblsp. vegetable oil
1/4 cup melted butter	1/4 cup carob powder

Place cookie crumbs in medium bowl. Drizzle melted butter and vegetable oil over top; using fork, blend together till crumbs are completely moistened.

Spray a 10 inch pie pan with non-stick vegetable oil spray coating. Press crumbs firmly onto bottom and sides of pan. Bake in 400 degree oven 8-10 minutes; checking through baking so as not to scorch edges.
Yields 1 - 10 inch pie crust

CAROB FLAKY NUT CRUST

Preheat oven 375 degrees (for prebaked crust)

1/2 cup pecans, chopped very fine	dash salt
3/4 cup whole wheat flour	1/4 cup vegetable oil
1/4 cup carob powder	

Place all ingredients in small bowl. Mix with pastry blender to fine crumbly mixture. Sprinkle 1 to 2 tablespoons water over mixture just till holds together. Press into 9 inch pie pan or onto bottom and 1 inch up side of 9 inch springform pan. Fill with desired filling and bake as directed; or for prebaked pie crust bake in preheated 375 degree oven 10-15 minutes or till lightly browned.
Yields 1 - 9 inch pie crust

Flaky Nut Crust Variation: Follow recipe for carob flaky nut crust except use 1/2 cup whole wheat flour and 1/2 cup all purpose flour and omit carob powder.

SPICY SNAP CRUST

Made with **spicy carob squares** for a quick and easy crust

Preheat oven 400 degrees

30 Gingersnap cookies
3 **spicy carob squares**

Break cookies into pieces. Place in a food processor container. Add carob squares. Process about 30-60 seconds, till even, moist, crumbs. Mixture will hold together when pressed. Press firmly into 9 or 10 inch pie plate. Bake in preheated 400 degree oven, 8 to 10 minutes. Cool and fill as desired.
Yield 1 pie shell

CAROB WAFER CRUMB CRUST

Preheat oven 375 degrees

4 cups 1 & 1/2 inch crisp carob cookies crushed to equal 1 & 1/2 cups	4 tblsp. melted butter 1 tblsp. vegetable oil

Place cookie crumbs in medium bowl. Drizzle metled butter and vegetable oil over top and stir to moisten with fork. Lightly spray non-stick coating over a 9 inch pan. Press crumb mixture onto bottom and sides of pan. Bake in 375 degree oven for 10-15 minutes or till lightly browned.
Yields 1 - 9 inch pie crust

Wafer crumb crust variation: Make carob wafer crumb crust, previous page, using any crisp vanilla wafer cookie crumbs.

Helpful Tip: to press crumbs into pie pan easily, place crumbs into correct size pan without pressing, making sure to ease crumbs higher around the edges of pie plate. Then take a pie pan which is 1 inch smaller than the one with crumbs, and set it into crumbs in first pie pan. Press gently but firmly into bottom and easily around edges. When you remove the top pie pan your crumbs will be pressed perfectly smooth into the pan.

EASY FROZEN CAROB CRUST

A cookie-like crust, you make in advance then bake when you're ready.

1/4 cup sugar	1/2 cup carob powder
1 & 1/2 cups all	1 cup coarsly chopped nuts
purpose flour	1 tblsp. vanilla extract
1/2 cup bran (raw),	1 cup cold butter, cut
use wheat or oat	in 1/2 inch cubes

In a food processor container, place sugar, flour, bran, carob powder, nuts and vanilla, cover; process 30 to 60 seconds to make powder mixture. Turn off machine and stir powder down from sides of container. Cover again and process, adding butter cubes one at a time. Process till mixture clumps together, about 30 to 45 seconds.

Tear off a 12 inch square of clear plastic wrap. Lay over 7 x 3 inch loaf pan and slightly press into pan, letting edges of plastic wrap hang over edges. Spoon dough into plastic lined pan. Press evenly to form smooth rectangle shape. Fold excess plastic over top to seal. Place in freezer for 1 hour. When frozen, remove from freezer, turn frozen, wrapped, rectangle onto a 12 inch square of aluminum foil, wrap, label and place back in freezer till ready to use. Freeze up to 2 months.　　　　Yields 2 pie crusts

Preheat oven 375 degrees

Instruction to prepare:

Slice ten - 1/4 inch slices (2 & 1/2 inch length of pie dough) for one 9 inch pie shell; or fourteen - 1/4 inch slices (3 & 1/2 inch length of pie dough), for one 10 inch pie shell. Arrange evenly on bottom and sides of 9 or 10 inch lighly greased pie pan. Gently press squares together to form shell. Flour fingertips. As dough thaws it will become softer and slightly sticky. Bake in 375 degree oven for 12 to 15 minutes or till lightly browned. Cool before filling.

For filling that needs baking, do not prebake, fill with desired filling and bake as directed in filling recipe. If edges brown too quickly cover crust rim with foil and continue baking.

Note: You may omit bran from recipe.

EASY FROZEN ALMOND CRUST

The same cookie-like texture, and the same convenience as **easy frozen carob crust**.

1 cup almonds	use wheat or oat
1/3 cup sugar	1 cup butter, cut
2 cups all purpose flour	in 1/2 inch cubes
1/2 cup bran (raw),	1 tblsp. almond extract

Place almonds in food processor first; add sugar, flour and bran. Process 30-60 seconds till almonds are chopped fine through mixture. Stop and stir down sides through processing. Cover and process again, adding butter cubes, one at a time till butter is blended into mixture evenly. Stop and stir down sides once or twice, to insure even distribution of butter. Turn into large bowl; stir in almond extract and 2 to 3 tablespoons water, just till mixture will form ball. Don't over mix.

Tear a 12 inch square of clear plastic wrap and place over 7 x 13 inch loaf pan, slightly pressing wrap into pan, let wrap hang over edges. Spoon dough into lined pan, press evenly in pan to form a smooth rectangle. Fold excess plastic wrap over top to seal. Place in freezer 1 hour. When frozen remove from feezer and turn onto a 12 inch square of aluminum foil, (leaving wrapped in plastic wrap), wrap with foil, label and place back in freezer till ready to use. Freeze up to 2 months.   Yields 2 pie crusts

Preheat over 375 degrees

Instructions to prepare:

Slice ten - 1/4 inch slices (2 & 1/2 inch length of pie dough) for one 9 inch pie shell; or fourteen - 1/4 inch slices (3 & 1/2 inch length of pie dough), for one 10 inch pie shell. Arrange evenly on bottom and sides of 9 or 10 inch lightly greased pie pan. Gently press squares together to form shell. Flour fingertips. As dough thaws it will become softer and slightly sticky. Bake in 375 degree oven for 12 to 15 minutes or till lightly browned. Cool before filling.

For baked filling, do not prebake, fill with desired filling and bake as directed in filling recipe. Check crust edges through baking time; if browns too quickly, cover edges with foil.

Note: You may omit bran from recipe.

SPECIAL CHEESECAKE CRUST

Preheat oven 400 degrees

1 cup all purpose flour
1/2 cup whole wheat
    pastry flour*
1/4 cup sugar

1/2 cup plus 3 tblsp. butter
1/2 tsp. lemon extract
1 egg

In small bowl combine flours and sugar, stir together. Cut butter into 1/2 inch cubes. Using a pastry blender, cut butter cubes into flour mixture until resembles course crumbly mixture. Sightly beat egg with lemon extract. Pour all at once into crumb mixture and mix just till forms a smooth ball; don't over mix or pastry will be tough.

Using a 9 or 10 inch springform pan, remove ring from the bottom section; set aside. Lightly grease bottom piece and press 2/3rds of dough evenly to edges, reserving remaining dough. Bake bottom crust 8-10 minutes or till very lightly browned. Cool. Prepare the filling.

To assemble crust and pan for filling:

Carefully fasten the ringform section of pan to bottom section, which has baked crust. Using reserved dough, press around bottom of ring, sealing at baked crust edge and coming up sides of pan 2 & 1/2 to 3 inches, (2 inches in 10 inch pan).   Yields 1 - 9 or 10 inch springform crust

Fill crust with filling and bake as directed.

*Note: If using regular whole wheat flour, sift twice.

EASY FROZEN ALMOND CRUST & EASY FROZEN CAROB CRUST PREPARED FOR FREEZING recipes on page 87 & 88

HONEY CAROB CHEESECAKE recipe on page 92

7

CHEESECAKES & CHILLED DESSERTS

CAROB CHEESECAKE DELUXE

Not too sweet, but 'oh' so rich!

Preheat oven 400 degrees

1 - 9 inch pastry dough
28 ounces cream cheese,
   room temperature
4 large eggs

6 **caroboil squares,**
   room temperature
2 tblsp. vanilla extract
1/2 cup honey

Line bottom and 1 inch up sides of a 9 inch springform pan with pastry. Bake in 400 degree oven for 5-10 minutes, just to dry top of crust. Remove from oven. Cool about 10 minutes.   Turn oven down to 325 degrees.

Place the cream cheese, eggs, carob squares and vanilla into a food processor container. Process till velvety smooth; about 60 seconds. Carefully pour mixture into a medium to large mixing bowl. Stir the 1/2 cup honey into carob-cheese mixture. Mix till completely blended together.

Pour carob-cheese mixture into slightly cooled, prepared crust. Bake in 325 degree oven for 1 hour & 15 minutes to 1 hour & 30 minutes, or till puffed and softly set in center. Remove from oven and place on rack to cool for about 1 hour. Gently slide a sharp, thin knife around inside edge of ring to loosen sides of cake from pan sides; remove ring. Leave cheesecake on bottom section of pan. Place on plate, cover and chill about 4 hours before serving.

When chilled, top with almond butter cream recipe (see index) if desired.

HONEY CAROB CHEESECAKE

Preheat oven 400 degrees for crust

1 Special cheesecake crust (see index)

Prepare the crust, using a 9 or 10 inch springform pan. Bake bottom section as directed; set aside to cool while preparing cheesecake filling. Leave oven on. The oven needs to be hot and then turned down as soon as cheesecake is put in.

Cheesecake filling:

2/3 cup milk	1/4 cup brown sugar
2/3 cup carob powder	3 eggs
1/2 tsp. orange extract	12 ounces cream cheese,
1 tblsp. vanilla extract	room temperature
1/2 cup honey	8 ounces cottage cheese

Combine all filling ingredients in food processor container. (Container fill line should hold 4 & 1/2 to 5 cups.) Process 60 to 90 seconds or till smooth and creamy.

Butter inside of ringform section of pan; carefully fasten bottom section, with cooled crust, to ring section. Press the reserved portion of dough, (from crust recipe), onto ring section, overlapping dough at baked crust edge to seal sides and bottom crust together, pressing dough up sides of pan 2 inches.

Carefully pour cheesecake filling into pastry lined pan. Place in oven and turn oven temperature down to 325 degrees. Bake for 1 hour & 15 minutes to 1 hour & 30 minutes. Top will be puffed and shiny, center will be set. Cool for 30 minutes. Place pan on plate. Use a sharp knife to loosen edges of cheesecake from ring. Carefully remove ring from cheesecake. Leave cheesecake on bottom section. When cooled, refrigerate at least 4 hours before serving.

DOUBLE CAROB CHEESECAKE

Carob crust and carob cheesecake — irrestible!

Preheat oven 375 degrees

easy frozen carob crust
  (see index for recipe)
10 ounces cottage cheese
4 eggs
3 rounded tblsp. cornstarch

4 carob cream squares,
  room temperature
10 ounces cream cheese, softened
2 tsp. vanilla extract
1 cup sugar

Slice 14 to 15 - 1/4 inch slices of frozen carob crust. Line sides and bottom of 9 inch springform pan with slices. Press together going up sides of pan 2 inches, to form evenly pressed crust. Bake in 375 degree oven for 10 minutes. Remove from oven, turn oven down to 325 degree. Set crust aside for a few minutes. Prepare filling.

Blender Method:

Combine cottage cheese, eggs and cornstarch in blender container. Blend until smooth and thick, stopping and scraping sides down once or twice, process will take 2-3 minutes to get mixture creamy smooth. Pour into large mixing bowl; add carob squares, cream cheese, vanilla and sugar. Beat till creamy - smooth consistency.

Food Processor Method:

Place all ingredients into processor container. Container will be full to maximum fill line. Process till smooth and creamy; about 60-90 seconds.

Pour mixture into still warm, prepared crust. Bake in 325 degree oven 1 hour and 30 minutes or till top is completely puffed and browned. Turn oven off and leave in oven for 1 more hour. Remove from oven and finish cooling on counter. Using a thin sharp knife, slide knife gently around edges of pan ring to loosen cheesecake from pan. Carefully remove ring. Leave cheesecake on bottom section, set onto plate. Refrigerate 4 hours before serving.

Variation: Make your favorite vanilla or lemon flavored cheesecake and use easy frozen carob crust for crust.

BLUEBERRY ICE CREAM DESSERT SQUARES

Preheat oven 350 degrees

1/2 cup butter or margarine
1 cup whole wheat flour
1/2 tsp. salt
1/2 tsp. nutmeg
1/2 cup brown sugar

1/3 cup carob powder
2 eggs
1/2 cup honey
1/4 cup flour
1 cup frozen blueberries, undrained

1 quart vanilla ice cream

In medium bowl combine butter, whole wheat flour, salt, nutmeg, sugar and carob powder. Cut together with pastry blender to fine crumbly texture. Set aside. Place eggs, honey, 1/4 cup flour and blueberries into a blender container. Process till thoroughly blended, about 30 seconds. Pour into a 12 x 8 inch well buttered baking dish or pan. Sprinkle crumb mixture over top and slightly press crumbs into blueberry mixture, leaving top crumbly. Bake in 350 degree oven 25-30 minutes; center will be set when done. Cool completely. Cut into 4 inch squares. To serve place blueberry squares on top of ice cream squares on serving plates; see below.   Yields 6 servings

To make ice cream squares:
Remove ice cream from freezer for 30 minutes. When slightly softened, press all of ice cream into 12 x 8 inch baking dish. Refreeze for at least 1 hour Cover for longer freezing time. Cut ice cream into 4 inch squares.

Variations:

Raspberry Ice Cream Squares:
Substitute 1 cup frozen raspberries for the blueberries.

Cherry Ice Cream Squares:
Substitute 1 cup frozen cherries for the blueberries.

TOFU CAROB CHEESECAKE

A light, smooth texture with a touch of orange flavor

Preheat oven 350 degrees

1 recipe **special cheesecake crust** (see index)
2 cups crumbled tofu*
2 cups cottage cheese
1 cup honey
3 **carobutter squares,** room temperature

3 **lite carob squares,** room temperature
dash salt
2 tsp. vanilla extract
1 tsp. orange extract
1/4 cup cornstarch

▶

Prepare special cheesecake crust: set aside

Place all ingredients in large bowl or preferably an 8 cup measuring container with pour spout. Stir together by hand to evenly distribute ingredients. Pour 1/2 at a time in blender or food processor container and process till creamy smooth. Remove to separate bowl; repeat with remaining mixture. Pour into prepared pastry lined pan. Bake in 350 degree oven for 1 hour & 30 minutes. Center will be set when done. Allow to cool about 30 minutes. Place pan on a plate. Using sharp knife, carefully loosen edges of ring and remove. Cover loosely, refrigerate overnight for best flavor. Garnish with mandarin orange segments.

*Note: Tofu can be found in the produce section of your grocery store. It is a cheese made from soy bean whey.

SPECIAL BANANA PUDDING

Brownies on the bottom of an irresistable old favorite

Preheat oven 350 degrees - brownies
400 degrees - meringue

1/2 recipe for **carob honey rum brownies** (see index)
4 medium bananas
Pudding:

1 & 1/2 cups milk	1 rounded tblsp. butter
1/2 cup powdered milk, dry	1/2 tsp. vanilla extract
1/4 cup cornstarch	1/2 tsp. banana extract
1/3 cup honey	1 tblsp. dark rum, optional
2 eggs, separated	Meringue, (recipe follows)
1/2 cup milk	

Prepare 1/2 of recipe for brownies. Pour batter into a greased 2 quart casserole dish. Bake in 350 degree oven for 20 to 25 minues. Set aside. Prepare pudding. In medium saucepan combine the 1 & 1/2 cups milk, milk powder and cornstarch. Using wire whisk stir till cornstarch is dissolved. Place on medium heat, stirring constantly, add honey. Cook till mixture thickens. Place egg yolks in small bowl; beat slightly. Stir several tablespoons of hot mixture into yolks, stirring quickly. Add egg yolk mixture back to hot mixture in saucepan; stirring briskly with whisk. Cook about 1 minute longer, till mixture bubbles and becomes very thick. Add the 1/2 cup milk; stir till smooth. Remove from heat, add butter, extracts and rum. Slice bananas. Place banana slices evenly over top of baked brownies in casserole dish. Pour pudding over bananas. Top with meringue, forming peaks. Brown in 400 degree oven about 10 minutes.
Yields 8 servings

▶

Meringue

2 egg whites
1/8 tsp. cream of tartar

2 tblsp. sugar
1/2 tsp. vanilla extract

Beat egg whites and cream of tartar on high speed till frothy. Add sugar, 1 tablespoon at a time. Add vanilla. Beat to stiff peaks.

SWEET CAROB ALMOND SQUARES

Almonds make it crunchy, the carob topping makes it irresistibly delicious!

Preheat oven 350 degrees

1 unbaked pastry for 10 inch pie:

Press pastry dough on bottom and 1 inch up sides of 8 x 8 inch square pan.

Carob cream topping:

2/3 cup scalded warm milk,
   (not hot)*
6 **sweet carobutter squares,**

room temperature
1 tsp. almond extract

Place warm milk in blender container. Cover and begin processing on high speed. Add almond extract and carob squares through top lid of blender. Process till smooth and creamy, about 30 seconds. Pour into bowl, cover and refrigerate 1 to 2 hours, till well chilled. Meanwhile prepare filling.

Almond Filling:

1/4 cup brown sugar
1/2 cup honey
1 tblsp. flour
1/4 cup melted butter,
   or margarine

3 eggs
1/2 tsp. vanilla extract
1/2 tsp. almond extract
3/4 cup chopped almonds

In mixing bowl, beat sugar, honey, flour, butter, eggs and extracts, on medium-high speed till smooth. Sprinkle almonds over crust in square dish. Carefully pour honey-egg mixture over almonds. Bake in 350 degree oven 45 minutes, or till top is slightly browned and puffed. Cool for 1 hour or till no longer warm. Top with chilled Carob Cream Topping; spread evenly to edges. Cover and chill 4 hours or overnight. Topping will be softly set and creamy. Cut into 2 inch squares.   Yields 16 servings

*Note: If milk is too hot or boiling, carob will be grainy.

CHERRIES ON A CLOUD DESSERT

This beautiful, light and flavorful dessert makes an excellent choice to serve after an elegant meal.

Carob crumb crust (see index for recipe.)
Prepare crust ahead in 10 inch springform pan. Bake according to recipe, cool and chill.

2 envelopes unflavored gelatine	1 cup milk
1/2 cup water	1 tsp. cherry extract
1/3 cup honey	3 cups cottage cheese
1/3 cup carob powder	2 egg whites
2 egg yolks	1/4 cup sugar
Cherry Topping, recipe follows	1/2 tsp. cherry extract

Sprinkle gelatine into 1/2 cup water, let stand 5 minutes. After 5 minutes, heat in microwave for 35 seconds, or in small sauce pan on low heat, to dissolve gelatine. In a food processor container combine the dissolve gelatine, honey, egg yolks, carob powder, milk and 1 tsp. cherry extract. Process till smooth, about 30 seconds. Carefully remove 1 cup of carob mixture from food processor container; reserve. To mixture left in food processor, add 1 & 1/2 cups of the cottage cheese. Process till light and smooth, 30 to 60 seconds. Remove this mixture to large bowl. Place reserved 1 cup carob mixture into processor with the remaining 1 & 1/2 cups of cottage cheese; process. Pour this mixture into bowl with first mixture and mix together well. In a seperate bowl, beat egg whites on high speed till frothy. Add 1/4 cup sugar, 1 tablespoon at a time. Beat in cherry extract. Beat to soft peaks. Using wire whisk, gently fold this soft meringue into carob-gelatine mixture. Mixture will be light and smooth. Pour into prepared crust. Smooth top with spatula. Place clear wrap over springform pan, making sure wrap doesn't touch filling. Chill 1 hour.

Prepare Cherry Topping:

16 ounce package frozen dark cherries
1/4 cup frozen cherry juice concentrate
1 rounded tblsps. unflavored gelatine

Place frozen cherry juice on cherries in medium bowl; let stand in warm place to thaw. (Don't heat) When thawed, but still cold, drain juice from cherries. Should equal about 1/2 cup. Sprinkle gelatine over juice, let stand 5 minutes. Heat in microwave for 40 seconds, or in small saucepan on low heat, to dissolve gelatine. Let cool 2 minutes. Stir gelatine mixture into cherries. Place in refrigerator 10 - 15 minutes; just till juice thickens to consistency of unbeaten egg whites. Carefully arrange cherries over chilled dessert. Cover and chill overnight. Next day carefully slide a thin knife blade around edge of ring to loosen dessert. Remove ring gently, leaving dessert on bottom section of pan; place on serving plate. Serve with whip cream. Refrigerate till serving time.

FROZEN CAROB DESSERT SQUARES

An easy dessert you make with instant pudding and whipped topping. Children like these on hot summer days.

Preheat over 375 degrees

6 - 1/4 inch slices **easy frozen almond crust** (see index)
4 **honey lite carob squares,** room temperature

1 small package instant pudding, (4 serving size)
2 cups cold milk
8 ounces frozen dessert topping

Place crust slices evenly on bottom of 10 x 6 inch baking dish. If frozen too hard, let stand 5 to 10 minutes for easier handling. Press evenly over bottom of dish. Bake in 375 degree oven about 15 minutes or till lightly browned. Cool completely.

Let carob squares come to room temperature. Have frozen topping in refrigerator instead of freezer, for easier mixing. In deep bowl, beat carob squares. Add pudding mix and milk, gradually, beating on low speed. When mixture begins to thicken beat 1 minute longer on high speed. Turn mixer to low setting; add whipped topping and just beat till light and smooth. Pour into prepared crust lined dish. Cover, place in freezer about 4 hours. Remove from freezer 30 minutes before serving. Cut in 2 inch squares. Serve semi-frozen. Yields 15 servings

Cover tightly and refreeze any leftover squares.

CAROB CREAM FREEZE

Carob ice cream, better than "bought"!

1 & 1/2 cups scalded milk
3 egg yolks, beaten
5 **carob cream squares**
1/2 cup honey

dash salt
2 & 1/2 cups light cream
1 tsp. vanilla extract

Place hot scalded milk in blender container. Cover and process on medium speed, adding egg yolks, carob squares, honey and salt through top chute of blender container. Process till well blended. Pour mixture into 2 quart container, with cover. Add light cream and vanilla. Beat together. Cover, refrigerate 4 hours or overnight. Liquid measure equals 5 cups; will make 1 & 1/2 to 2 quarts ice cream. When chilled, place in ice cream freezer container of your choice. Freeze according to manufactures instructions.
Yields 1 & 1/2 - 2 quarts ice cream

For special treat, serve with warm bittersweet carob sauce (see index for recipe).

PUMPKIN DREAM DESSERT

Creamy, light and flavorful pumpkin filling, over **carob gingersnap crust** and topped with a delicate meringue pudding

Carob gingersnap crust (see index for recipe)

Pumpking Filling:

1 pkg. unflavored gelatine	1 & 1/2 tsp. vanilla extract
2/3 cup sugar	1 tsp. ground cinnamon
1 egg yolk, reserve egg	dash ground cloves
white for meringue	dash ground nutmeg
1 cup milk	8 ounces cream cheese,
1 cup pumpkin	room temperature

Meringue pudding:

2 cups milk	2 tblsp. butter
1/3 cup sugar	1 tsp. vanilla extract
2 egg yolks, reserve egg	ground cinnamon
whites for meringue	for garnishing
3 tblsp. cornstarch	Meringue (see recipe below)

Prepare crust: Preheat oven 400 degrees. Press crumbs into a 2 quart casserole dish, pressing up sides of dish 2 inches. Bake in 400 degree oven for 8 minutes. Cool, set aside.

To make filling: In medium saucepan, place gelatine and sugar. Stir together. In small bowl beat egg yolk and milk together. Add to gelatine-sugar mixture in saucepan and stir to mix. Let stand 3-5 minutes. Place on low heat. Stir constantly till gelatine dissolves and mixture slightly thickens; about 5 minutes. Remove from heat. Stir in pumpkin till smooth. Add vanilla and spices. Pour mixture into mixing bowl. Beat in cream cheese till light and smooth. Chill till mixture thickens; about 1 hour. Meanwhile, prepare Meringue Pudding.

To make pudding: Place milk and sugar in saucepan. On medium heat, heat just till mixture begins to bubble, stirring constantly. Remove from heat. In small bowl stir egg yolks and cornstarch till thick, lemony colored. Remove 1/4 cup hot mixture and quickly stir into yolks. Stir back into hot mixture in saucepan. Heat on medium heat till bubbly and thickened, about 5 minutes. Remove from heat. Add butter and vanilla. Set aside. Prepare meringue. Partia lly fold meringue into pudding, leaving meringue in clumps throughout pudding. Set aside.

To make meringue: Using three reserved egg whites; beat till foamy, add a dash of cream of tartar. Beat to soft peaks. Sprinkle in 2 tblsp. sugar; beat to stiff peaks.

Prepare Dessert: Spoon thickened pumpkin into prepared crust. Carefully spoon pudding over top, taking care not to mix two layers together. Chill about 6 hours. Spoon into dessert bowls.   Yields 8-10 servings

Top to bottom:
BANANA CAROB RIPPLE BREAD, page 107
ALMOND FUDGE FILLED PILLOWS, page 104
QUICK NUT ROLL, page 107

CAROB WHEAT BREAD, page 101

8
BREAD & SWEET ROLLS

CAROB WHEAT BREAD

A moist and flavorful yeast bread

Preheat oven later 350 degrees

1 cup warm water	1 tsp. orange extract
1/4 cup honey	1 tsp. salt
2 pkgs. active baking yeast	1 beaten egg
1/4 cup dry milk powder	1/4 cup vegetable oil
3 heaping tblsp. carob powder	4 cups whole wheat flour
warm water	1 cup all purpose flour

Place 1 cup warm water in large bowl with honey. Add yeast; let stand 5 minutes to dissolve. In a 1 cup measure, place milk powder and carob powder. Add water to equal 1 cup. Pour into large bowl. Add orange extract, salt, egg and oil. Mix together well. Add 3 cups of whole wheat flour, one cup at a time, mixing well after each addition. Beat several minutes to a smooth, sticky dough. Let stand at room temperature 45 mintues.

By hand, stir in remaining whole wheat flour. Dough will start becoming stiff. Place all purpose flour onto flat surface. Place dough on top of flour, flour hands, knead 5-8 minutes, adding more flour if necessary, till no longer sticky and dough is smooth and elastic. Place in oiled bowl, turning dough so top surface is oiled. Cover; let rise in warm place till doubled, about 1 hour.

Punch dough down; divide in 2 equal portions. Roll each piece into a 12 by 8 inch rectangle. Roll up jelly roll fashion. Pinch seam, tuck ends under. Place in well greased 9 x 5 inch loaf pans. Cover; let rise till doubled, about 1 hour. Bake in 350 degree oven 35-40 minutes.
Yields 2 - 9 inch loaves

CAROB SWIRL BREAKFAST ROLLS

These rolls are exceptionally moist, and so very good

Preheat oven 350 degrees

2 pkg. yeast	1 tsp. orange extract
1/2 cup warm water	1/3 cup vegetable oil
1/4 cup hot milk	3 eggs
1/2 cup honey	2 cups whole wheat flour
1 tsp. salt	2 & 1/2 cups all purpose flour

Carob filling, recipe below
Carob-orange glaze, recipe below

Sprinkle yeast over the 1/2 cup warm water, let stand 5 minutes. In large mixing bowl blend together hot milk, honey, salt, orange extract, oil and eggs. Stir in the 2 cups whole wheat flour and mix 1 minute. Add the dissovled yeast; stir well. Begin stirring in the 2 & 1/2 cups all purpose flour, 1/2 cup at a time. Dough should form stiff ball in center of bowl as you stir; about 1 more minute. Cover bowl and let dough rise in warm place about 1 & 1/2 hours. Punch dough down, knead into smooth ball and divide into 2 equal pieces. Let dough rest 5 to 10 minutes. Roll first piece out into a 10 x 12 inch rectangle. Brush with 1 tblsp. cooled, melted butter. Spread 1/2 of **carob filling** (below) over entire surface. Starting at narrow end roll up jelly roll style, pinch seam to seal. Repeat with remaining dough & filling. Using a sharp knife cut rolls into 1 & 1/2 inch slices. Place cut sides down into well greased 9x13 inch baking pan. Let rise 45 minutes or till doubled. Bake in 350 degree oven for 25 minutes or till lightly browned. Cover with foil and last 5 minutes of baking time if rolls brown too quickly. Leave in pan and cool. Spread Carob-orange glaze over tops of rolls. These rolls are best when completely cooled.

Carob filling:

4 **carob cream squares,** room temperature	1 tblsp. flour
1/3 cup honey, slightly warmed - not hot	

In small bowl mix with spoon till smooth and creamy.

Carob-Orange glaze:

4 **carob cream squares,** room temperature	1 tsp. orange extract
1/4 cup honey	

In small bowl, mix till well blended and smooth.

Yields 15 large rolls

CAROB BRAN ROLL DOUGH

Basic sweet carob dough for making filled rolls

1/4 cup warm water
  (110-115 degrees)
1 pkg. active dry baking yeast
1/2 cup butter or margarine,
  melted, cooled
1/3 cup honey
1/2 tsp. salt
1/2 tsp. orange extract

2 tsp. grated orange peel
3/4 cup warm milk
1 egg
3/4 cup bran
1/2 cup carob powder
1 cup whole wheat flour
1 & 1/2 cups all purpose flour

Dissolve yeast in warm water. Let stand 5 minutes. In large mixing bowl, beat together butter, honey, salt, orange extract, grated peel, milk and egg. Beat till well blended. On low speed, add dissolved yeast; blend in. Add bran, carob powder and whole wheat flour. Beat 2 minutes on low speed. Stir in enough of remaining flour to make stiff-sticky dough. Dough should form sticky ball. Place in large greased bowl, turning once so greased side is to top. Cover and refrigerate at least 2 hours or overnight. Dough will begin to rise in refrigerator; check periodically and punch down. Remove dough from refrigerator about 3 hours before serving time. Punch down and shape as desired in filling recipes given.
Yields 1 recipe for sweet dough variations, page 104-105

SWEET ROLL DOUGH

Basic sweet dough for making filled rolls

1 pkg. baking yeast
1/4 cup warm water
1 cup hot milk
1/4 cup butter or margarine
1/3 cup sugar

1 tsp. cinnamon
1 tsp. salt
1 egg
3 & 2/3 cups all purpose flour

Soften yeast in warm water for 5 minutes. Place butter in hot milk until butter melts. Pour into large mixing bowl. Add sugar, cinnamon, salt, egg and dissolved yeast. Beat on medium speed of electric mixer 1 minute. Add 1 & 1/2 cups of flour. Beat on medium speed 3 minutes. With wooden spoon, stir in remaining flour. Stir till all flour is dissolved and mixture is stiff and sticky. Rub 1 tblsp. vegetable oil onto sides and bottom of deep, glass bowl. Spoon dough into oiled bowl, shape into a ball; turn dough over to oil top. Cover bowl with oiled plastic wrap. Refrigerate 2 hours or over night. Will make 10 large rolls.
Remove dough from refrigerator about 3 hours before serving. Punch dough down and shape and fill as desired in filling recipes given.
Yields 1 recipe for sweet dough variations, page 104-105

FILLING & SHAPE VARIATIONS

SPICY FILLED LOGS:

1 recipe - **sweet roll dough**
   or **carob bran roll dough**
4 **spicy carob squares,**
   room temperature
3 tblsp. flour

3 tblsp. bran
3 tblsp. wheat germ
1/3 cup date sugar
2 tblsp. vegetable oil

In small bow, mix together all filling ingredients. Using 1/3 cup dough for each log; press dough into 4 inch circle. Spread heaping tablespoon filling over circle to 1/2 inch from edge. Roll circle up jelly roll fashion. Pinch seams to seal. Repeat with remaining dough and filling. Place on greased baking sheets. Let rise till doubled, about 1 to 2 hours, depending on how long dough has been at room temperature and how warm kitchen is. Bake 375 degrees 12-15 minutes. Drizzle with carob or powdered sugar icing.   Yields 10 to 12 logs

ALMOND FUDGE FILLED PILLOWS:

1 recipe - **sweet roll dough or carob bran roll dough**
1/2 recipe **almond carob carmel filling** (see index for recipe)

Using 1/3 cup dough for each pillow, press into 4 inch circle. Spread each circle with 2 tablespoons filling to 1/2 inch from edge. Bring edges up to meet in center, forming a little sack. Pinch together, well, to seal in filling. (If not sealed, filling will ooze out as it bakes.) Place on greased baking sheet. Let rise till almost doubled. Bake 350 degrees 12-15 minutes. Drizzle with powdered sugar icing or carob icing.   Yields 10 to 12 pillows

CREAMY CAROB SWIRL:

1 Recipe - **sweet roll dough or carob bran roll dough**
1 cup **creamy carob filling** (see index for recipe)

Roll dough into 12 x 15 inch rectangle. Spread filling to 1 inch of edges, evenly over dough. Roll up jelly roll fashion, pinching at seams to seal. Fold ends under, towards seam side. Place on greased baking sheet, seam side down. Let rise till doubled. Bake in 350 degree oven, 30 to 40 minutes. Will be browned on top and when tapped will sound hollow. If browns to quickly, cover loosely last 10 to 15 minutes with foil tent. Cool, drizzle with carob icing or sprinkle with sweet powder (see index for recipe).   Yields 1 swirl loaf

CAROB PECAN CRISPS

1 recipe - **sweet roll dough**
　　or **carob bran roll dough**
3 tblsp. melted butter

1/3 cup brown sugar
3 tblsp. carob powder
1 tsp. ground cinnamon

Mix butter, sugar, carob powder and cinnamon together till well combined. Set aside. Roll dough out to 12 x 15 inch rectangle. Spread butter-sugar mixture over dough evenly over dough surface. Roll up jelly roll fashion, starting with long edge. Pinch edges to seal. Cut roll into 1 inch slices making 12 rolls. Place rolls on greased cookie sheets about 3 inches apart. Place a sheet of wax paper over tops or rolls. Using a rolling pin, roll over wax paper covered rolls, flattening rolls to 1/2 inch thick circles. Remove wax paper. Let rolls rise 1 to 2 hours,' till doubled. Rising time depends on how long dough has been at room temperature and how warm room temperature is. When rolls have doubled, place wax paper over tops again and roll flat to 1/8 to 1/4 inch thick. Remove wax paper. Brush rolls with 1/4 cup melted butter. Combine: 1/2 cup granulated sugar, 1/2 tsp. ground cinnamon and 1/3 cup chopped pecans. Sprinkle this mixture over buttered rolls, evenly. Place wax paper over tops one more time. Roll flat. Bake in 400 degrees 10-15 minutes or till crisp and browned. If crisps brown too quickly, lower oven temperature to 375 degrees. Cool.
Yields 12 crisps

CAROB NUT ROLL

1 recipe - **sweet roll dough**
　　or **carob bran roll dough**
1/4 cup milk
1/2 cup honey

2 **carobutter squares,**
　　room temperature
2 tsp. vanilla extract
2 cups coarsely ground nuts

Mix together milk, honey, carob squares and vanilla in small bowl till well mixed. Stir in nuts. Set aside. Roll dough into 12 x 15 inch rectangle. Spread honey-nut mixture evenly over dough to 1/2 inch from edges. Roll up jelly roll fashion, starting at long edge. Pinch seams to seal. Place seam side down on greased cookie sheet. Let rise 1 to 2 hours, or till doubled, depending on how long dough has been at room temperature and how warm room is. Bake in 350 degree oven 35 to 40 minutes, till lightly browned. Glaze or sprinkle with sweet powder (see index for recipe)　　Yields 1 - 12 inch nut roll

CAROB ANISE & RAISIN STOLLEN

This stollen is flavor enhanced with orange and anise

Preheat oven later 350 degrees

Yeast dough:

1/4 cup honey	1 egg yolk, reserved
1 cup warm milk	for filling
2 pkgs. active baking yeast	grated rind of 1
1 cup sourdough*	orange (3-4 tblsp.)
2 cups whole wheat flour	1 tsp. orange extract
3 cups all purpose flour	1/2 tsp anise extract
1 whole egg	1/4 cup vegetable oil
1 egg white	2 tsp. salt

Stir together honey and warm milk; sprinkle yeast over top, let stand 5 minutes. In large bowl beat together whole egg and egg white, orange rind, extracts, oil and salt. Add yeast mixture. Beat in sourdough and whole wheat flour. Beat for 1 minute. By hand stir in all purpose flour, 1/2 cup at a time, saving last 1/2 cup for kneading. Stir for 1 minute. Place the last 1/2 cup flour onto board or kneading surface. Turn dough out onto board. Knead for 5 minutes. Dough should form smooth ball. Grease a large glass bowl and place dough in greased bowl, turning so greased side is up. Cover and let rise in warm place for 1 to 1 & 1/2 hours. Prepare the filling.

Carob Anise Raisin Filling:

2 **lite carob squares**,	1 tsp. vanilla extract
room temperature	1/2 tsp. anise extract
1/4 cup honey	1 tsp. anise seeds
2 tblsp. molasses	1 egg yolk, (reserved)
2 tblsp. flour	1/2 cup raisins
1 tblsp. melted butter	

In small bowl mix all ingredients, except raisins, till smooth. Add raisins. Punch dough down. Place on lightly floured surface. Roll dough out to 18 x 12 inch rectangle. Spread 2 tblsp. of soft butter over surface; spoon filling over top. Spread evenly to 1 inch from edges of dough. Roll up jelly roll style, starting at narrow end. Pinch seam and tuck ends under. Brush top with 1 tblsp. butter and sprinkle with anise seeds. Place in well greased 15 x 10 inch baking pan. Let rise in warm place 1 hour or till doubled.
Preheat oven 350 degrees. Bake 35-40 minutes. Cool; sprinkle with powdered sugar.
Yields 1 large stollen

*Note: In place of the sourdough, you can mix together 3/4 cup flour, 3/4 cup water and 1 tblsp. lemon juice, stirred to make think paste like mixture.

BANANA CAROB-RIPPLE BREAD

Preheat oven 350 degrees

3 ripe bananas
1 cup sugar
2 egg whites
1/4 cup plain yogurt
1/4 cup vegetable oil
1/2 tsp. vanilla extract
1/2 tsp. banana extract
1 tsp. baking soda

1/2 tsp. baking powder
1 cup all purpose flour
1/2 cup whole wheat flour
1 tsp. ground cinnamon
1/4 cup bran
1/2 cup chopped pecans
1/2 cup **creamy carob filling**
   (see index for recipe)

Mash bananas. Place bananas, sugar and egg whites in large mixing bowl. Beat together till well mixed. Add yogurt, oil and extracts; beat in. Stir baking soda into banana mixture. In separate bowl, combine baking powder, flours, cinnamon and bran. On low setting, beat dry mixture into banana mixture just to moisten and mix. Stir in pecans. Pour 1/2 batter into well greased and floured 9 x 5 inch loaf pan. Spoon creamy carob filling down center of batter in pan. Pour remaining batter over top. Using the handle of a wooden spoon-gently swirl carob filling through banana batter, not touching sides or bottom of pan. Bake in 350 degree oven for 50-60 minutes, or till tests done. Cool in pan 30 minutes. Remove to rack to finish cooling. Serve with whipped cream cheese or just plain.   Yields 1 - 9 inch loaf

QUICK NUT ROLL

This sweet pastry-like treat is quick and easy because you use refrigerator crescent roll dough to make them.

Preheat oven 350 degrees

1 cup chopped pecans
1 cup chopped dates
1/3 cup honey
1/4 cup melted butter
   or margarine

1 **lite carob square,**
   room temperature
2 tsp. vanilla
1 - 8 ounce pkg. refrigerator
   crescent rolls

In medium bowl stir together pecans, dates, honey, melted butter, carob square and vanilla. On lightly floured surface, roll out crescent roll dough into rectangle. Gently press preforated seams together to seal dough rectangle. Spoon pecan mixture evenly down center; starting at narrow end, spoon filling down long length of dough. Fold one side of dough over filling, then fold other side over top. Pinch seam, place seam side down onto greased 15 x 10 inch cookie sheet. Dot top with butter. Bake in 350 degree oven 25-30 minutes. Carefully, using two spatulas, one at each end of roll, remove to rack to cool. When cooled sprinkle with powdered sugar, or sweet powder (see index for recipe).   Yields 1 nut roll

CAROB STREUSEL COFFEE CAKE

Preheat oven 350 degrees

4 **carobutter squares,**
   room temperature
1/2 cup brown sugar
1 tsp. baking soda
dash salt
2 tsp. cinnamon

1 tsp. vanilla extract
1 cup applesauce
1 egg, slightly beaten
1/2 cup raisins
1 cup whole wheat flour
1/2 cup all purpose flour

Combine all above ingredients; mix till well blended. Pour into greased and floured 8 inch square baking pan. Top with topping mixture, below.

Topping:

1/2 cup brown sugar
1/4 cup carob powder
2 tblsp. flour
1/2 tsp. cinnamon
1/4 tsp. nutmeg

1/4 tsp. ginger
1/3 cup butter or margarine
2 tblsp. molasses
2 tblsp. bran
1/2 cup chopped pecans

Using pastry blender or fork, combine topping ingredients in small bowl till crumbly. Sprinkle over batter. Bake in 350 degree oven 30-35 minutes, till lightly browned and cake tests done. Cut in 2 inch squares; serve warm or cold. Yields 16 streusel squares

EASY STICKY BREAKFAST BUNS

Preheat oven 375 degrees

So good warm from the oven!

1/4 cup brown sugar
1/4 cup butter or
   margarine, melted
1 **lite carob square,**
   room temperature

1 tblsp. dark corn syrup
1 tsp. vanilla extract
1/2 coarsely chopped pecans
1 - 10 ounce can, flaky
   refrigerator biscuits

In small bowl, mix together brown sugar, butter, carob square, corn syrup and vanilla. Spoon into greased 8 inch round cake pan, spread evenly to edges. Sprinkle pecans over top. Place biscuits over top of mixture in pan. Bake at 375 degrees, 15-17 minutes, till well browned. Remove from oven and turn onto serving plate immediately. Scrape any remaining topping in pan over tops of buns. Serve warm.   Yields 10 sticky buns

INDEX